HOW TO RAISE A MORE
Creative Child

HOW TO RAISE A MORE Creative Child

by Larry and Marge Belliston

Argus Communications
Allen, Texas 75002 U.S.A.

This book was prepared at Information Design, Inc., with the help of the following individuals:
 Larry Belliston—Producer/Director
 Kurt Hanks—Director
 Jay Parry—Editor
 Jill Moffat—Typist

Special thanks to the following parents for their assistance:
 Alan and Mary Lou Arveseth
 Ron and Judy Hammer
 Randy and Vickie Morgan

The children's artwork and some related experiences were provided by the Belliston children:
 Troy (age 7), Brock (age 5), and Dion (age 4)

FIRST EDITION

Copyright © 1982 by Information Design, Inc.
All rights reserved. No portion of this book may be reproduced, stored in a retrieval system, or transmitted in any form by any means—electronic, mechanical, photocopying, recording, or otherwise—without prior permission of the publisher and copyright owner.

Printed in the United States of America.

Publisher:
Argus Communications
A Division of DLM, Inc.
One DLM Park
Allen, Texas 75002 U.S.A.

International Standard Book Number: 0-89505-077-3
Library of Congress Number: 82-70044

9 8 7 6 5 4 3 2

Table of Contents

Starting Out Right 1
Creating "On Demand" 5
Abstraction 7
Too Much Freedom 10
Getting in a Rut 12
Kinds of Junk 14
Reading 15
3-D Thinking 17
Picture This 18
Convergent Thinking 21
Brainstorming 23
Switching Things Around 25
Kinds of Tools 27
Experiences and Creativity 28
Combining Things 30
Hatching an Idea 31
Checklists 33
Hunches 35
Getting It Down 36
Experts and Specialists 37
Adaptation 39
Positive Approach 42
A Sense of Destiny 44
Learn to Question 45
Division and Omission 47
Small Rewards Can Cause Creativity 49
Need Fosters Creativity 50
The Real Solution 52
Complex or Simple? 53
Divergent Thinking 54
Develop Holistic Thinking 56
Trading One for Another 57
Dreams 59
Mother Nature and a Good Idea 61
Order and Tradition 63
Turning Things Around 65
Games and Puzzles 67
Adding To 68
"Great Job!" 69
Seeing It in Your Mind 71

Hard Work	73
Accept the Unpredictable	75
Multiple Skills	76
Don't Take Things Too Seriously	78
Preconceptions	79
"I Can't!"	81
Modification	83
Environment Promotes or Kills Creativity	85
Playing Around	87
Modeling	90
Drawing	92
Aim for One, Hit Another	94
Individuality	97
Don't Scare Them Away	99
The Real Problem	101
Rest and Relaxation	103
Metaphorical Thinking	105
Object Analogy	106
Defer Judgment	108
What If?	109
Hobbies and Fine Arts	111
Discovery Can Lead to Creativity	112
Making It Real	114
Taking Away	116
Concentration	117
Communicating and Creativity	118
Ideas Trigger Other Ideas	120
Respecting the Child	121
Art, Dance, Music—and Creativity	123
Multiplication	125
Honesty	127
Emotional Climate	129
Point of View	131
Ask First, Judge Later	132
Family Influence	134
Summary Checklist	136
Answers	143
Bibliography	144

Starting Out Right

There's a real mystique about creativity in our society. To hear writers and artists and musicians talk, they've been able to tap into some secret force in the universe.

Of course, that's not the actual case at all. Creativity is a *skill*—and it can be learned by anyone. It's true that some people have more natural creative abilities than others. But usually a person is more creative than others because he's learned the skill better. Some people haven't learned the skill at all—or it was trained out of them as they grew up.

This book contains principles, methods, and ways to be more creative. It also tells about many of the personality traits of creative individuals. By knowing and applying these principles and methods, and by promoting those personality traits, parents can more easily help their children develop natural creative abilities.

Kids Are Full of It

Kids are naturally creative. They're born with the ability to question, dream, wonder. They haven't learned the molds that force us into the "logical" solutions to problems, and because of that they're willing to try anything.

Certainly everything a child does isn't creative. And he probably won't manifest his creativity in the same way an adult will. But he will bring creativity and innovation and freshness into many things he does in life. He may not be a great artist, but he will look at the world with new ideas. He may not learn how to be a great inventor, but inevitably he will make some inventions on his way to solving problems in his life.

We parents often unknowingly stifle the creative potential of our kids. Even our public education system is set up in such a way that it tends to kill creative potential. There the teacher will emphasize

habits
daily routines
set schedules
rote memorization

multiple choice answers to questions
true-false answers to questions
forms

All of these discourage creativity. They encourage sameness and conformity, rather than unique and innovative approaches to life.

Don't expect a lot of help from your local school system as you try to help your child improve his creative skills. Schools have to set up systems that make things easier—they do this by making all children adhere to easily managed daily routines and rules. Each parent is on his or her own when it comes to creativity. But the picture isn't as bleak as it may seem. Because there is a lot a parent can do. Parents have the child, virtually without outside interference, for the first five or six years of the child's life. After that the schools get involved—but for only six hours out of the child's waking fifteen.

But how do you go about helping your child be more creative? If you sit the child down and say, "Okay, let's have another creative session," you'll probably fail miserably. We think it's simpler than that anyway. It's best simply to be familiar with good creative approaches and skills, and then to use them *at the opportune moment.*

One at a Time

Any one idea in this book, if the child comes to understand it, will do a great deal toward helping him to be creative. Don't think you have to use every idea. Each child will have areas of strength; it's best just to focus on those.

If a child were to become proficient at any one of the creative techniques in this book, that may be enough. Edison was probably the greatest inventor the world has ever seen. He was especialy good at the approach of *experimentation*—but not especially good at many others.

Einstein was a master of *visual thinking*. That's why his creations almost always dealt with dimension like time and movement and energy.

Mozart got his creative ideas through *abstraction*. But he would have been lost with drawing or visual thinking.

How do you know which approaches to encourage with which of your children? The best answer is just to get to know the techniques and get to know your children. We have a good friend who has eight kids—and no two of them are alike. He has

a competitor
a dreamer
a helper
a dancer
a nice guy
an inquisitive girl
a tenacious one
a baby!

You might have the same kind of variety with your children. Each child has a different dominant trait or personality. And in a similar way each child has a different kind of creative potential.

Does it all sound too complicated? It's not. We think that as you read the different topics in the book you'll see how easy it is to apply them. We believe that simple things work best. And so we've tried to make the book as simple as possible.

The Creative Family Habit

One thing that will help in dealing with children is to form the habit of creativity in the home. We try to be accepting of creative behavior, even if it's messy.

Parents who have fun with their kids are generally more tolerant of creative behavior. Hence their kids are more likely to be creative. The ability to play is an important part of developing creativity.

Logic is important and essential in our society—but it's only half the person. The other half is the creative side, and it's as important as the logical. Kids who have both are better off.

But it's the parents who can cause creativity to happen. It's not likely to come from the schools. It's not likely to be encouraged outside the home. So try doing "different" things in your home, regularly. Seek new and creative ways to do things with your children. It's not *work* to be creative, it's *fun*.

Creating "On Demand"

"You ought to see the cute drawings Johnny does," bragged Dad to one of his friends. "He makes them on the spur of the moment. He always has a pad and pencil in his hands. The one of me reading the newspaper last night was a riot. I should have brought it to show you."

Later that week the friend dropped by. "Hey, Johnny," Dad said, "make one of your little drawings like you do all the time." Everyone looked at the boy expectantly. Johnny just stood there.

"I'd really like to see one," the friend said.

Pause.

"Johnny?" Dad said.

Johnny looked at the pencil and pad and then at Dad and then at the floor. "I can't."

"What do you mean, you can't?"

"I don't know," said Johnny. "I just can't."

When a child is put on the spot where he *has* to come up with something creative, chances are he won't perform. **You can't force or demand creativity.** You'll just inhibit it. Pressure to be creative restricts the freedom of thought that must precede creativity.

Trying to force a child to be creative is like putting his head in a vice—it doesn't do a lot of good, and it can do a great deal of harm.

An experiment was recently conducted on a college campus where students were paid to find creative solutions. If they were successful, they got the money. If they weren't they lost out. The students under that kind of pressure were much less successful than were those who were simply given the problem as an interesting challenge.

Things Parents Can Do

A parent can set the stage for creativity to happen, but he or she can't get it by demands and force. That only stifles creativity. Set the stage by being open and accepting. Whether the child performs to our expectations or not, we should accept what he's done. If he feels free to fail as well as to succeed, he'll be a lot more prone to develop his creative abilities.

Abstraction

"Look at my town," said Jimmy to Dad. "This is the store. This is the school. This is the church, and these are the houses." He pointed to various structures he had made out of Legos plastic pieces.

"What are these straight things between the buildings?" asked Dad.

"Those are the sidewalks," said Jimmy.

"And what are these?" Dad pointed to several small pieces.

"Those are the cows on the farm," Jimmy said proudly. "And these are the tractors and these are the chickens."

Jimmy was using the creative skill of *abstraction* by using the Legos as building materials. The more a person is able to see abstract qualities in things, the more he'll be able to find creative solutions. This is because **making logical or creative connections is easier at the abstract levels than at real levels.** As a child learns how to make those abstractions, he learns more and more how to be creative.

The mediums that seem to be the most creative are those that are the most abstract. The artist starts with meaningless colors and combines them in a creative way to make a picture unlike any that have been made before.

Abstraction is a common and useful form of creativity. The creative person takes something concrete and puts it into a new form.

The composer of music takes abstract symbols of musical notation and combines them to create new melodies and harmonies.

The dancer uses her body as a means of expressing emotions and events abstractly.

The writer takes the abstract symbols of the alphabet and transforms them into a new poem, an essay, or a novel. Or a book like this.

All these disciplines are creative because they take the abstract and turn it into the concrete. Here's an example of how it can work. The following letters are an utter abstraction.

a b c d e f h i l m n o r s t y

Yet they can be used to say "Mary had a little lamb" or "Many men eat crabs." You can create "To be, or not to be," or "The bell tolls for thee," whichever you wish. The abstraction is a tool the creative person can use to accomplish his ends.

Creativity becomes easier when one starts looking at things in the abstract. For example, for centuries doctors had difficulty understanding the heart. Then a scientist viewed it in the abstract and realized it was just a pump. After that, it was a simple step to move from the abstraction to a creative result: researchers were able to develop an artificial heart.

The writer learns to use the abstract alphabet and thus develops his ability to express himself creatively. The scientist becomes more creative as he gains facility with the abstract.

If you wanted to find a creative solution, you'd find it helpful to go back to the abstract. Suppose you wanted to design a lightweight item you could carry with you to use as an emergency covering if it got cold. It would serve you like a heavy coat would, or like a roof to protect you from the weather. What could you carry with you?

The first step is to consider a roof in the abstract—what does it do? What is its function? It's a covering. What other kinds of coverings are there? Rugs, coats, clothes, tents, plastic wrap, aluminum foil, umbrellas, spray paint.

It's now possible to buy a new kind of foam insulation in spray cans. The insulation is designed to be used in buildings and the like. But why couldn't a foam be designed for a person to spray on himself to protect himself from the cold?

By going back to the abstract you've found a possible solution to your problem. Certainly many other solutions could also be found. At this point we've only opened the door!

Things Parents Can Do

A parent can have abstract elements around the house for children to use. Some excellent choices are blocks, Legos, Lincoln logs, Erector sets, pieces of cloth, and the like.

Parents can let children make things with common household items. For example, a pile of frozen peas or marshmallows, coupled with a batch of toothpicks, becomes an excellent abstract element for creating.

You might want to practice seeing things in abstract elements yourself. Then you can broaden the range of your children's comprehension and help *them* to see the abstract in things.

The more a parent can help a child to see in the abstract, the more the parent will be able to help the child be creative.

For example, you could view things around the house in the abstract sense of function. Thus, if you were looking for fasteners, you'd realize that a button fastens clothing together, pins fasten, a doorlatch fastens the door to the frame, a thumbtack fastens a paper to the wall.

Too Much Freedom

Some parents give their children a lot of freedom. "We like to really give our Matthew his head," they say. "That way he can realize his creative potential to the fullest."

Other parents are strict and limiting. "No kid of mine is going to run wild and make messes all over the house just so he can feel creative!"

Which is best? How much freedom should a parent give his creative child? Do you let him run crazy and do whatever enters his little head? Do you set strict limits? And if you do set limits, will that stifle his creativity?

All through this book you'll find suggestions about how to help your child develop his creativity. Many times I'll tell you not to be worried about messes, not to stop your child when he's creating.

But don't misunderstand. I'm not advocating permissiveness! More appropriate would be *controlled freedom*. The child is not free to do whatever he wishes. But neither is he afraid to lift pencil to paper.

Everyone does better with limits. **Setting limits will actually enhance creativity.** Limits won't cause creativity, of course—but they will improve its quality.

Let me give you an example. Suppose you call an interior designer on the telephone. "I'd like you to design me a nice room," you say. "Give it your best shot." He may indeed try to do a good job. But the designer's work won't be nearly as good as if he had a few limits. Maybe he included antique furniture. You hate antiques. Maybe he spent $5,000. You only had $1,000. Maybe he put an expensive pool table right in the middle of the room. But it's not a game room.

Oh-oh. Try again. This time give your designer some limits: "I'd like you to design me a nice room," you say. "It's our formal dining room. Pick out some nice contemporary dining-room furniture, and cover the walls mainly in blue. You only have $1,000 to work with."

Now the designer's work will be more appropriate. And you

can bet he'll be more creative too. Because he knows just what parameters he'll be working with.

These kinds of limits are what the real world is made up of. The child whose parents permissively allow him to do whatever he wants will have a rude awakening when he finally leaves home. Creativity functions best under limits. And that's how it will *have* to function when the child grows up.

Things Parents Can Do

It's rainy outside. Stanley whines about having nothing to do. But mom's busy; she can't spend her day entertaining Stanley. "Go play!" she says.

Stanley goes to play. But there are too many options. Stanley can't make up his mind. He gets bored; flits from one thing to another. His play is very much less than creative.

Next door. It's rainy outside. Nan whines about having nothing to do. But Nan's mom is busy too. She gets down a bunch of colored pencils and a stack of paper—and sets limits. "Draw *ten* different things using only these pencils."

Nan starts to draw. Their house. Mommy. Daddy. A family portrait. Some trees.

She looks out the window. Still raining. Now she starts to stretch. She starts to get a little more creative. She draws an elephant. A girl jumping rope. Three men in a tub. Oscar and Big Bird from Sesame Street. A castle.

With his lack of limits, Stanley really didn't get anywhere. But Nan drew all kinds of neat things. It was her limits that made the difference.

When parents want their children to be creative, they shouldn't just turn them loose. It's much better to set a few limits. To have some rules. By setting up a situation and then having the child create within those constraints, parents won't be stifling. They'll be enhancing!

And the parents will get one nice added bonus: the kids will be restricted in their messes!

Getting in a Rut

Before putting a ham in the oven for Christmas dinner, a young wife cut off both ends. "Why did you do that?" her husband asked. "I don't know. That's how my mother always did it."

The whole family was at the young couple's home for Christmas, so they went into the living room and asked the wife's mother. The answer: "Because my mother did it."

The grandmother was also there for the holidays. "Grandma, why did you cut off both ends of the ham?"

Grandma thought a minute, then said, "When I was first married, we had such a small oven that all meats had to be cut a certain size to fit." It was such a habit that it carried into the third generation.

Habits are fine in many ways. But there's one problem when it comes to childrearing and habits: **Habitual ways limit creativity.**

Here's a puzzle to test habitual thinking. Cut out four pieces of paper to match the shapes of those shown, then arrange them as I have them in the picture. Try to make a square by moving only one of the pieces of paper. It's possible—but only if thinking is not habitual. (For answer, see the Answers page at the back of the book.)

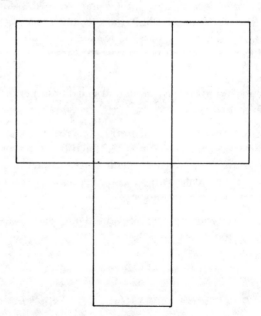

With a habit, a person does the same thing over and over again. Yet creativity involves finding new and different solutions. When we form habits of doing things certain ways, we feel no need to seek better solutions. After all, the habits are more comfortable.

The problem grows when habits are passed from parent to child. The child picks up the habits of his parents and adds a few more of his own. His life may be ordered and predictable—but it's also uncreative.

Things Parents Can Do

Encourage your children to do things in a different way. Help them to try new ways of making beds or other chores, in order to break the routine of "habitual living" which limits creativity. One mother encourages her boy to rearrange his bedroom furniture (bed, small desk, dresser, and toy box) every month. He comes up with some "weird" (says mother) but creative ways of putting his furniture and looks forward to changing things each time.

It also helps if Mom and Dad break some routine habits themselves. For example, when coming home from the store, go by a different route each time, instead of the same old way. Go to Grandma's house by a different road. Change the seating arrangements at the dinner table. Vary menus. Try new recipes. Have pizza for breakfast instead of cereal or eggs. The object is to break habits, to have an atmosphere of innovation in the home. Innovation leads to creativity.

In short, make a "habit" of doing things in a variety of ways. This "habit" of varying things will eliminate the other kind of habit which is to do the same things over and over again.

Another test: Take two pieces of string (each about 32 inches long) and tie them to your wrists and to those of a friend, hooking yourselves together as shown. Now, without breaking or untieing the strings, untangle yourself from your friend. Think creatively and you may be able to do it! (For answer, see the Answers page at the back of the book.)

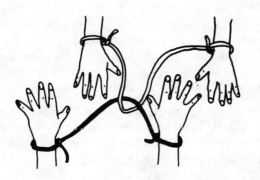

Kinds of Junk

Junk increases creativity! **The more material a child has to work with, the more creative he can be.** And junk is a great source of materials.

Here is a list of some of the junk kids love:

wire	clothes pins	wheels
sticks	paper clips	popsicle sticks
tape	pieces of cloth	old spoons
writing materials	string	springs
boxes	glue	toothpicks
buttons	paper	old boards
pipe cleaners	fasteners	cardboard

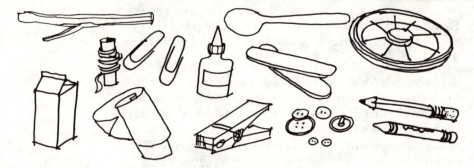

Things Parents Can Do

Some parents let each child have a place in his room where he can collect or store his own "junk." A box, a drawer, or a shelf does nicely. The important thing is that he has a *place*.

Another good idea is to establish a central location in the house where these types of things can be stored. All the children go there for something they might need. One family keeps a drawer in the kitchen, another a box in the family room. With such a junk place, the children can create when they want to; they don't always have to bother you for tape or glue or whatever. They know it's "in the drawer."

If you set up a junk drawer, you may also want to establish some ground rules. Children need to clearly understand what's allowed and what's not. When they break a rule, just withdraw the privilege for a while.

Reading

We all have great memories from childhood. But almost invariably some of the best are from stories we read or heard.

"Once upon a time there was a great giant. . . ."

"When Alice in Wonderland saw the White Rabbit go down the hole, she became very curious. Why did the rabbit go down the hole? And why was he wearing a vest? . . ."

"The little dog laughed to see such sport, and the dish ran away with the spoon."

And the inevitable questions:

"Mommy, are giants really in the world?"

"Daddy, how can a rabbit wear a vest?"

"Mommy, why did the dish run away with the spoon?"

Stories and poems are great for the imagination. They take a child from the world he's in every day and transport him to a new one, one with magic, or glamour, or mystery, or a feeling of exotica, or a place of just plain fun.

Some kinds of reading can promote creativity and imagination. As children get older and learn to read and like to read, it can be a real boon to creativity. They learn the information necessary to be able to create. And they are motivated by the experiences, environments, or creations of others. Those who aren't old enough to read can be read to. They can also "read" the pictures and create their own stories. And after parents read to their children, the children can retell the stories in their own words.

The following list shows some of the kinds of reading that can promote creativity:

Short stories are good because they leave so much to the imagination. Also you can think up your own endings if you don't like the one written, or if you want to leave it off for your child and ask him or her to make one up.

National Geographic type of magazines are good because they talk about people in different lands and show how they solve their problems by using approaches different from the ones your child is used to. You may want to simply look at the pictures with your child, explaining what each is about.

Biographies discuss people's lives and bring to mind divergent thinking. They show how others have approached problems with uncommon solutions. Biographies of creative people—inventors, musicians, philosophers, etc.—can particularly motivate your child to be more creative.

Popular Science, Popular Mechanics, Mechanix Illustrated, and the like can stimulate your child to want to create things on his own, to get started with different solutions. It also helps them to envision different ideas that could be developed. "Future magazines," such as *Omni* and *Next*, are also good for older children.

Reading is so effective in stimulating the mind that often kids like to read even before they know how to read!

3-D Thinking

Structural imagery is the ability to see the third dimension. With structural imagery you're able to envision real or imagined objects either on paper or in the mind. **This skill of structural imagery enables people to be creative**. When inventing specific objects, they can "see" in their minds exactly what the object will look like, how much space it will take up, and so forth.

Things Parents Can Do

You may want to take three-dimensional drawings and help your child to see the three dimensions.

Or use the reverse principle. Show your children a three-dimensional object such as a box and have them envision it folded, squashed, flat, etc., and then draw it in the two dimensions. This helps to reinforce the third-dimension concept and the concept of structural imagery.

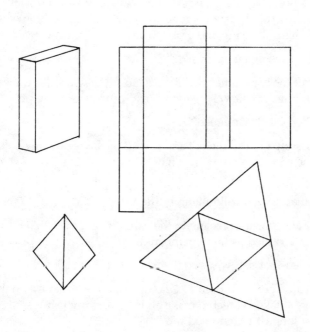

Remember those aptitude tests you took when you were in high school? Such tests always ask the student to take a flat object and visualize it three-dimensionally, as I've shown in this example. Why do experts test those skills? Because they show creative abilities, for one thing.

Picture This

"Dad! Dad!" yelled Brent. "Me and Grandpa caught a fish 10 feet long!" Brent raced through the front door clutching his fishing pole.

"That's a big fish, Brent. Tell me . . ."

"And I fell in the water and Grandpa saved me and . . ."

"Hey, slow down! Where did you and grandpa go?"

"We went to the big fishing hole—the one with the broken tree by it."

Dad frowned, trying to remember which tree Brent was talking about.

"You know, Dad. The tree you said lightning had broken down the middle."

Dad smiled. "Okay, I know the one you mean. The tree is split in two. Isn't there a log or something that goes out into the water?"

"It's not a log, it's a long, skinny rock. And you can walk out on it to fish. That's where me and grandpa were fishing when I got this pull on my line. I was so surprised I fell in the water."

"Why were you surprised?"

Brent looked a little sheepish. "Cause I was watching these two boys on the other side instead of watching my pole."

"Then what happened?"

"Grandpa pulled me out and helped me hang onto my pole. I almost lost it. And then I'd have lost the fish too. Then I started pulling in the fish."

"What do you call pulling in the fish?"

"Grandpa calls it reeling in the fish. It was a big fish!" Brent's eyes sparkled as he remembered.

"A ten-foot fish you said," added Dad.

"Yeah," breathed Brent. "Grandpa said it was almost an inch long. It takes 12 feet to make an inch, and my fish was almost that long. It tasted good too."

As Brent told about his fishing trip, he was using reproductive imagery—which is recalling a situation or an object in exact minute detail. **This ability to visualize mentally is a vital skill in creativity.** When Dad was helping Brent describe his experience, he was helping him to develop a creative technique.

Even very young children can picture things in their minds. Here's an example of how the picture came out on paper. It's obvious what the picture's of, right? An Indian peeking out of a teepee!

One reason Albert Einstein was able to develop the theory of relativity was that he worked on visualizing it. He recognized that the ability to picture things in the mind is vitally important to the creative process.

At one point he was having difficulty with one aspect of his theory. As was his practice, he sought a creative solution

19

through visualizing. He pictured himself in a cage that was being pulled through space at a rapid rate. In his hand was a ball—which he let go.

Then came the question: did the ball drop to the bottom of the cage, or did the floor of the cage rise up to meet it? Through clarifying the image in his mind, Einstein was able to come to a workable conclusion.

Novelist James Michener writes books by using a similar approach. He likes to go to the setting he's going to use in his book. As he sits in the setting, say a Hawaiian jungle, he describes it in his own words. Then he visualizes his characters as they walk and talk in the setting. It's Michener's ability to imagine things in detail that makes his novels as popular as they are.

One of the greatest inventions ever was the electric motor, developed by Nikola Tesla. Tesla imagined the motor in absolute detail before he ever wrote his design on paper. He tells of walking in Budapest with a friend when some of the problems with his design resolved themselves in his mind. He stopped, picked up a stick, and drew the answer on the sand, showing his friend what the motor would look like. His ability with the motor and with other inventions he made came through his skills of visualization.

Things Parents Can Do

As children learn to mentally record or picture exact details, the creative potential increases. One game that enhances imagery skills is the "tray game." The game is played by putting several items on a tray. A person looks at the tray for a short time—say for about one minute. Then the tray is removed and he is to describe in detail what was on the tray. The person with the best memory wins.

A variation of the game is to look at an object such as a butterfly, caterpillar, flower, truck, building, or toy and then close your eyes and describe it in detail—all its properties, movements, colors, smells, and so on.

When a child has a fun or unique experience, he loves to tell someone about it. By listening to the story, a parent builds not only the child's self esteem, but also his creative visual imagery abilities. Both the child and the parent gain, as Dad did with Brent.

Convergent Thinking

See if any of this sounds familiar. You're working somewhere in the house, minding your own business—and you start to think the kids are being kind of quiet. And although you *like* quiet, it's usually a danger signal when it goes on too long.

In you go to the bedroom where they're playing. Oh-oh. Popcorn all over the floor. Three guilty faces look up at you.

"All right. What's going on in here?" you ask.

Molly talks fast. "We're playing wedding. Tina and Ross are the bride and groom and I'm the preacher."

Your hands are on your hips—but they're so little, down there below you. And kind of cute. Still you want to know the whole story: "So why in the world did you have to make a mess with the popcorn?"

"I couldn't find any rice," Molly says. "I needed *something* to throw when they got married."

It's convergent thinking that causes kids to use popcorn in place of rice at a pretend wedding.

"Why don't we go to Joey's house for our honeymoon?"

You've had things like this happen to you. I'm sure of it—it comes with the territory. And I'll tell you, nine-tenths of the time it's hard to keep cool. If you're like me, you want to do a little yelling; you want some action *fast*. The steam is building up inside. Somehow there has to be a release.

But then you think twice. Instead of giving your kids the word, you realize that they've taken another step toward creativity.

Molly doesn't know it, but she has just gone through *convergent thinking*. She wanted rice, but there wasn't any. Problem. So she quickly thought of what she might use to substitute. Solution: popcorn. **Convergent thinking is the ability to scan many relevant facts, then zero in on the correct solution to a problem.**

Convergent thinking works from many ideas down to one. Divergent thinking works from one idea out to many.

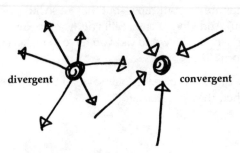

Think of what it takes to put together a puzzle. You have a hundred pieces all laid out in front of you. Which to choose? You scan the possibilities, narrow down the selection. Pull out three or four that might work.

Take a clear look. Pick the one that works. *Voila!*

Usually we think of creative thinking as free and easy. But convergent thinking is more judgmental. As such, it's an important part of reaching creative solutions.

Things Parents Can Do

Parents can help their children use convergent thinking by playing word games with them. They play the "I'm thinking of . . ." game, describing something while the others guess what they're thinking of. Or they pick a letter in the alphabet and see how many different words their children can think of that begin (or end) with this particular letter. Another game is the object tray. Children look at about 10 objects on a tray. When an item is removed, they try to identify what it was.

Brainstorming

"What do you want to eat at the picnic Saturday?" asked Mother. The ideas came thick and fast:

"Hotdogs!"
"Hamburgers!"
"Soda pop!"
And:
punch
potato salad
baked beans
corn on the cob
watermelon
carrot sticks
radishes
olives
pickles
potato chips

Kids can come up with different solutions to the same problem when they get together and brainstorm.

"We have quite a list of food ideas now," said Mother. "Can you think of what else we need to take with us?"

grill
charcoal and lighter fluid
paper plates and cups
napkins
silverware (plastic ones so we won't have to wash them)
barbeque forks and spatula
tablecloth for the table
picnic table—("You know, the fold-down one.")
newspapers
paper towels
matches
salt and pepper—("We forgot that in the food part.")
catsup and mustard and onions—("We forgot those too!")

This mother was using a creative technique called brainstorming: a question is asked and everyone thinks up as many answers or varieties as they possibly can in a given time. None of the ideas are judged—any answer even remotely pertaining to the subject is okay. Some ideas may be weeded out later, but in the planning session anything goes.

Brainstorming (which usually takes place in a group of two or more people) is a very helpful creative technique. One idea usually triggers another which in turn triggers another and so on.

Things Parents Can Do

Work together on brainstorming solutions to common concerns.

Remember that brainstorming is nonjudgmental.

If your child wants help on a particular problem, brainstorm to find the answer.

Brainstorming works a lot better when it's done according to the rules.

Rules for Brainstorming

1. Make sure everyone knows what you're going after.

2. Let everyone speak out his ideas; have someone assigned to write them down on a chalkboard or piece of paper.

3. Don't make a judgment on any of the ideas during the brainstorming session. That will kill the flow of ideas right off. Instead just write them down and judge them later.

Switching Things Around

One of the most famous pictures of all time is *Blue Boy*. Nearly everyone has seen and appreciated that painting. Not only was *Blue Boy* well done, but it was a pivotal painting in the history of art. Before *Blue Boy* was painted, artists typically used blue as a background color: they'd put it in the sky or mountains or something else in the background, but not in the person being painted. But the *Blue Boy* artist rearranged that approach and put blues right in the boy! His approach caused artists to look at their color combinations in a new way—simply by rearrangement.

We spend a lot of our lives rearranging things—moving furniture around (and back again), putting our hair up in a different way, putting clothes on in new combinations. In fact, we rearrrange things so much that often we don't even think about it. It becomes second nature.

Because we do it so much, rearrangement often isn't viewed as a creative process. And yet without it, we'd be unable to successfully make the changes we want to make. Rearrangement is invariably a creative act. **Considering rearrangement as an option is frequently an important step to getting creative ideas.**

New visual and graphic designs are accomplished by rearranging the elements into different patterns. Music is constantly *rearranged* to form new sounds. Architects *rearrange* structural elements and floor plans to create new building designs. Artists *rearrange* colors to produce various moods with their pictures.

John rearranges his furniture in his room every week. It exasperates his mother, but John's creative expression in his room results in a very neat room. And John is developing his creative abilities in the process.

Tom's father practices golf by hitting 30 golf balls into a vacant lot near their home. He used to pay Tom 1 cent for each ball retrieved. He usually got 27 or 28 of the 30 balls back. So he creatively rearranged the payment system. Tom got nothing for the first 27 balls, 5 cents for the 28th ball, 10 cents for the 29th, and 15 cents for the 30th ball. Tom got the same amount of money—30 cents—and dad got all 30 balls back every time.

Rearrangement can cause a person to come up with some crazy solutions—but a boot will keep your head dry in the rain!

Of course, Tom didn't get any more money from the new arrangement than he did at first. It was all designed just to favor dad!

But Tom will benefit, just by being around a dad that thinks like that. Tom will see the *rearrangement* way of thinking. And as he grows and matures he'll learn how to use it for himself.

In sports, a great coach can make a world of difference between a winning and losing team just by rearranging who plays where. When the coach makes a change, a parent could explain what's happened to his sports-fan child.

Recipes create new food dishes—some exciting, some plain, simply by rearranging the same elements. The same basic formula can be used to make pizza, hot rolls, and cinnamon twists. When you use rearrangement in your meals, on occasion describe what you've done.

"I'm not going to eat these peas," Cindy announced. "I *hate* them. She squashed them, threw them, hid them under the edge of her plate—did everything but put them in her mouth. One day, mother rearranged Cindy's plate. She put the food in the form of a clown face. Cindy quit playing with her peas and ate them. She wanted to eat the whole clown.

Things Parents Can Do

Parents can help their child be more creative by learning to rearrange ordinary items in his life, be it furniture, food, or ways of looking at things. The more a child rearranges things, the more skilled he'll become at using this creative technique.

Kinds of Tools

The more "tools" your child has access to the more creative he'll be. A list of the kinds of tools children need for creativity includes:

scissors
rulers
construction tools
hammers
pliers
screwdrivers
wrenches
chalk
chalkboard
needles
thread
sewing machine
crayons
paints
paint brushes
power tools
cutting tools
kitchen utensils
spoons
forks
egg beater
spatulas
cookie cutters
pans
bowls

Tools are important. But here's a fact of life that every parent might just as well face up to: Kids wreck tools. Does that mean we don't allow our kids to use any tools? Not really. A parent has two courses of action: Either recognize the potential hazard to the tools and let the child play with them anyway. Or let the child have his own tools. Whichever you choose, it will probably be a good idea to spend time with the child teaching him how to use and care for the tools so they won't be lost or broken.

Experiences and Creativity

The more experiences a person has, the more creative he's able to be. This is because creativity is often the combination of known elements. The more your child knows, the more he's able to combine!

Thomas Alva Edison was one of the most creative people of all time. One reason was the broad experience he accumulated in his life. Past experience gave him more raw material to work with.

Look at what Edison had experienced by the time he was twenty-two:

As a twelve year old he had traveled extensively on the railroads in his area, working on the trains selling candy and newspapers.

When the train stopped in Detroit, he spent hours on end reading in the city library.

As a fourteen year old he started his own newspaper.

By the age of nine he had read such sets of books as *The History of England, The Decline and Fall of the Roman Empire,* and *Natural and Experimental Philosophy.*

Throughout his youth he tried numerous experiments. He had his own chemical laboratory in the basement of his home.

He had invented and sold a stock ticker machine and had patented a vote recorder.

Another example of the power of experience on creativity can be seen in the music of the Beatles. After they'd been together for a few years their music began to change noticeably. Why? Because they'd been traveling the world, having new experiences. At one point they became interested in Far Eastern religion and music—and that experience showed up in their music, both in the instruments they used and in the melodies they composed.

Years later, they changed again. People listening to Paul McCartney today can see that he's the same musician who was so influential with the Beatles. Yet he's matured and grown since the group broke up, and his songs are markedly different.

Things Parents Can Do

Parents can encourage—allow—the child to do things that will give him a wide range of experience. Sometimes it's hard to let a child go, to allow him to have the freedom that is a prerequisite to learning experiences—but it needs to be done.

If you're like me, you sometimes want to hold them back. You know that going after new experiences makes a person vulnerable, that it opens them to hurt and failure. Yet experiences are essential. If you hope to have a creative child, you *must* allow him the freedom to experience new things.

It helps if a parent can be with the child during many of his experiences to help him *fully* experience the situation, to help him see things he might overlook, to explain things, to point things out, to answer (and ask) questions.

Here are a few activities that give a child good experience:

swimming	student government
singing	experimenting with computers
dancing	model kits
scouts	electronic kits
sports	woodworking
4-H	carving
art	musical instruments
crafts	music composition
camping	
nature walks	
trips to the library	
field trips: hospital, bakery, police station, fire station, etc.	
bedtime stories	
jogging with mom or dad	
a trip with mom or dad to work	
experiments in the kitchen	
writing poems and stories	
public speaking	

This drawing was done after a father-son nature walk (by the son, of course!).

Combining Things

Lots of things are made by combining other things:

- Some refrigerators have been combined with plumbing to dispense cold water.
- A disposal on the kitchen sink is a chopping and grinding machine combined with the normal kitchen plumbing.
- Motor homes are homes combined with wheels.
- A shower was combined with a tub (by some enterprising inventor) to have them both in one place.
- The motorcycle is a bicycle combined with a motor.

Creative ideas usually aren't all new—instead they're a combination of old or common things put together in a new way. **Creative solutions often come by combining seemingly unrelated elements.** Sometimes it works to look at one thing and transfer the principle to something else. For example, the idea of a squid's propelling movement was transferred to an airplane, creating jet propulsion aircraft.

The electric toothbrush is a combination of an electric motor and a toothbrush. Music and a computer combine to make a Moog synthesizer. Two lenses put into one pair of eyeglasses make bifocals.

A wind-up tank crocodile with saddle and CB—the result of combining.

Things Parents Can Do

Children will naturally combine unrelated items or ideas as they solve problems. Parents can help them see that's part of being creative. Some children enjoy trying new combinations in the kitchen. Give them that freedom, even though everyone doesn't always enjoy eating the creations. The key is to *allow* the creative combinations to occur.

Hatching an Idea

Hank, a friend of mine, was coming out of a store with another fellow when he saw his mother just getting out of her car. Even though it was raining, they went out to meet Hank's mother.

She got out of her car and put her umbrella up—but on the way up it caught on her hair, which was really a wig. The umbrella tore the hair from her head and flipped it into a puddle.

Hank calmly picked the wig up from the puddle, shook it off, and stuck it back on his mom's head. Then he said, "Well, mom, I can see you're busy. I guess we'll get out of your hair." And he left.

You've probably had experience with the great comeback. Someone is rude to you and you can't think of a thing to say back. Ten minutes later, after the opportunity is long gone, the perfect comeback pops into your mind. It came through incubation. Or you're trying to remember a person's name or maybe a tune. It just won't come and you forget about it. Then, the next day, out of the blue it comes to you. Incubation. You thought you forgot all about it, but your subconscious was hard at work searching through your memory files.

Hank had the perfect thing to say to his mother—and just at the right time. He didn't even have to wait for incubation. But usually we have to rely on the incubating process. It's an important creative technique.

Incubation is where the subconscious mind solves a difficult problem after you have stopped consciously trying to solve it. Most creative people use incubation—though many may not realize it. One writer smelled orange blossoms while in an old gothic church. Thick, high walls and orange blossoms ought to be a turning point in a story, he thought. Six years later a complete story came to him using those two elements.

I told you about Hank and his snappy comeback, which was apparently just waiting in his mouth to come out. Let me tell you about a more common experience, one that requires incubation.

Bernard Russell consciously used incubation in his work. He said: "I have found, for example, that if I have to write upon some rather difficult topic, the best plan is to think about it with very great intensity—the greatest intensity of which I am capable—for a few hours or days, and at the end of that time give orders, so to speak, (to my subconscious mind) that the work is to proceed underground. After some months I return consciously to the topic and find that the work has been done. Before I had discovered this technique, I used to spend the intervening months worrying because I was making no progress. I arrived at the solution none the sooner for this worry, and the intervening months were wasted, whereas now I can devote them to other pursuits."

You can help your incubation by using the following steps:

1. Concentrate and study about a problem.
2. After intense work, quit and give it to the subconscious.
3. Wait.
4. The idea will come. Realize it may take awhile. Then write down the answer so you won't lose it.

Things Parents Can Do

When your child is struggling with a problem, suggest he use the approach of incubation. Explain how it works and how he can apply it to his particular problem.

Most ideas come out a lot better if they're allowed to incubate.

Checklists

I don't know about you, but I'm absolutely lost without my lists. I make a list of my appointments for the day and keep it nearby. It helps me keep track of where I am and where I ought to be. It gives me a grip on the day.

My list makes a real difference in my ability to do things well.

I have other lists, too. Lists of people I want to see, lists of books I want to read, lists of ideas I hope to explore someday.

Along with all those lists, I always keep handy my creativity lists. I know that sounds a little weird, to have a creativity list. But a creativity checklist is just as valuable as any other list you could ever have. It helps you be more creative.

A creativity checklist helps me look at things from a lot of different angles. It works as a mind-jogger, just like my appointment list. It helps me make sure not to overlook any idea, or any source of an idea. A checklist helps me to consider ideas, concepts, strategies, and other points-of-view that I might otherwise forget about.

If you've ever gone shopping without your grocery list, you know exactly what I'm talking about. You walk down one aisle and pick up a few things, move on to the next, aimlessly, not sure of what you want or where to look. After a lot of wasted time and wasted steps you get to the check-out counter.

But when you get home you realize you forgot the most important thing of all!

With a list I don't have that problem. I can go through the store quicker and without forgetting anything.

An idea checklist is as helpful as a shopping list. It helps one cover the bases and avoid being sidetracked.

There are a lot of different kinds of checklists. Most of them don't have anything at all to do with creativity—and yet they can be used for that over and over again. Just about any kind of list will help a person look at his problem with a new point of view, and that's often all that's needed to get him going on a creative solution.

Here's one list I really like to use. It's called the manipulative verb list, and it has the following words in it:

☐ coat	☐ invert	☐ check
☐ search	☐ predict	☐ vibrate
☐ inflict	☐ flatten	☐ segregate
☐ transpose	☐ subtract	☐ eat
☐ copy	☐ soften	☐ release
☐ grow	☐ repeat	☐ rotate
☐ attract	☐ enhance	☐ fasten
☐ fluff-up	☐ separate	☐ complement
☐ connect	☐ manipulate	☐ focus
☐ organize	☐ stimulate	☐ destroy
☐ extract	☐ continue	☐ bend
☐ force	☐ visualize	☐ relate
☐ harden	☐ divide	☐ recheck
☐ multiply	☐ unify	☐ repel
☐ loosen	☐ build	☐ speed-up
☐ symbolize	☐ stimulate	☐ return
☐ inject	☐ contrast	☐ cycle
☐ attach	☐ reflect	☐ lighten
☐ squeeze	☐ adapt	☐ stamp
☐ delay	☐ display	☐ structure
☐ size	☐ shift	☐ distort
☐ define	☐ rethink	☐ bypass
☐ add	☐ retreat	☐ weigh
☐ coerce	☐ subdue	☐ tighten
☐ transform	☐ stretch	☐ concentrate
☐ cut	☐ verbalize	☐ coordinate
☐ blur	☐ insert	☐ eliminate
☐ reform	☐ freeze	☐ increase
☐ heat	☐ submerge	
☐ extrude	☐ thicken	

A checklist can make the difference between a mind in stall and one going sixty miles an hour.

Just how can parents use the above list for creativity? On a rainy day, for example, they can give their child a roll of aluminum foil. Then give the child the above list of manipulative verbs (or read it to him). Ask him to take the foil and do the things on the list to it. It's surprising how many creative ideas can come from just this one "task."

But remember this is only one list. Others can easily be "custom-made" to match an individual family's needs and to stimulate a particular child's creativity.

Hunches

Rick was making a go-cart. It was nearly done—but he was having difficulty hooking the steering column to the wheel assembly.

Then, out of the blue, he got an idea he hadn't had before. "If I hook this here," he told his friend, "it should work."

"How do you know?"

"Well, I just have a feeling."

Rick tried his idea—and it worked. He had been the happy recipient of a hunch.

Hunches or intuition are very important to creativity. Logic is a step-by-step thinking process from beginning to end. Hunches skip all the steps and jump to the end in one big leap. The person sees the final result (or complete idea) first. Then he can work back through the steps to verify the creative idea. Thus, **creative people cultivate hunches or intuition to help them with their creativity.** Hunches are one of the main processes of creativity.

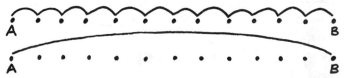

Usual thinking is to go from step to step, gradually progressing from point A to point B. But hunches can take a person from A to B in one great leap.

Sometimes kids get a leap of intuition—but before they can try the idea, their parents shut them down. "Don't bother with that idea. It won't work." The trouble is that the parent is thinking logically, while the child is thinking intuitively.

As far as creativity is concerned, Einstein claimed, "The really valuable thing *is* intuition."

Things Parents Can Do

It helps a child to have his parents listen to his hunches. This indicates to the child that having hunches must be a kind of thinking. If the parent thinks it is worth hearing about, the child assumes that what he is doing must be worthwhile. The child receives positive reinforcement that what he is doing is favorable.

Getting It Down

Creative people keep notes, drawings, sketches, and so forth to help them on their various creative projects. **If creative ideas are not recorded in some form, they will vanish.** They'll never become a finished creation or product. Changing the thought into something real—making a model, writing it down, drawing it out, talking it into a tape recorder—is a critical step in creativity. Making a record of the idea is the step that *must* occur before the idea can be translated to a final product—whether that product be a song, a machine, a new process, or whatever.

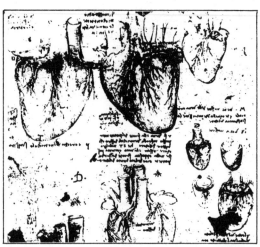

Leonardo da Vinci age 32   Brock age 5

Most creative people keep notebooks to record their ideas and their progress.

Things Parents Can Do

Some parents encourage journal keeping. This "habit" will help in the development of creativity as the child learns to record his thoughts and ideas. They set one night a week for journal recording in their family. The kids are asked to draw something that happened during the week, and mom or dad write the words the child dictates. Those old enough to print or write are encouraged to put their thoughts down verbally as well as to draw pictures.

It's also good to encourage children to make notes or drawings or models of their creative ideas.

Experts and Specialists

"Look at this cage I built for my gerbil," said eight-year-old Timmy excitedly.

Dad took a look. "It won't work at all," he said. "Look at the bottom. You can't clean off the droppings. There's only one little wire place. And see how crooked it is. Why, I'll bet the gerbil would squeeze right out between these two boards and run away."

Parents who continually belittle or criticize their children's ideas or projects stifle their children's creativity. We shouldn't expect our children to be experts in what they do. They just don't have the experience.

In fact, we shouldn't even *wish* they were experts. **"Experts" or "specialists" are often less creative than others—all they can see is the "one" approach.**

Maybe that sounds a little strange to say that experts are less creative. And yet in the very process of becoming an expert a person grows less and less creative. He becomes better and better in his field; he comes to know more and more how to do things. And the better he gets, the less he's interested in experimenting. As far as he can tell, he already knows the best approach to his work. Why should he seek new and creative solutions?

This attitude can be seen in the great innovations that periodically change our world. An incredible number of them come from *non*experts. For example:

The safety razor was invented by a salesman.

Kodachrome film was invented by a musician.

The ballpoint pen was invented by a sculptor.

The automatic dial telephone was invented by an undertaker.

The parking meter was invented by a journalist.

The pneumatic tire was invented by a veterinarian.

David Campbell points out that history records a long list of innovations that came from outside the "expert" organization. The automobile was not invented by the transportation experts of that era, the railroaders. The airplane was not invented by automobile experts. Polaroid film was not invented by Kodak; and digital watches were not invented by watchmakers. The list is endless; and the moral vivid.

Things Parents Can Do

Children will tend to become more creative if their parents allow them to make their own things, to make their own mistakes with their inventions and creativity. Maybe what the parents feel will be a mistake will be a new and different solution to the problem. A child will often come up with a simple and creative solution that the parent could not see because the experience of the parent caused him to overlook the obvious.

Kids don't care about experts. All they know is they're walking around with a big question or problem, and they need to get rid of it.

"He who has no inclination to learn more will be very apt to think that he knows enough."
—Powell

Adaptation

Mom used a new recipe to make a hamburger casserole. But it didn't taste just right. "Julie, what do you think this casserole needs?"

Nine-year-old Julie tasted the casserole. "It tastes flat. Maybe it needs salt."

Mom added a little more salt and they tasted it again. "It still needs something, Mom," said Julie.

"Maybe some garlic powder will help," Mom said. She added a bit.

"Now it really tastes good," said Julie.

"Yeah," Mom said.

When a person adapts existing ideas to form new ones, he's being creative. Mom adapted the recipe to make a whole new creation. Different people use adaptation to be creative in different ways. One mother who has run out of potatoes will serve gravy over bread. Another mother may have run out of both potatoes and gravy—she'll make a further adaptation: creamed corn over the bread.

Writers are constantly creative through adaptation. There are less than a dozen plots the novelist can choose from. But by adapting an available plot formula, the novelist can create an entirely new book.

Most jokes are adapted from earlier jokes. "Little moron" jokes became "ethnic" jokes, which became "elephant" jokes. New styles of clothing are invariably adaptations from an older era or from another culture or subculture.

Shakespeare once became enamored with an old Danish legend. He thought about it at great length—until finally he adapted it by writing the idea into a play. He called it *Hamlet*.

The music of "The Star Spangled Banner" was adapted from England's "God Save the Queen."

In 1939 two schoolteacher sisters, Mildred and Patty Smith Hill, were looking for a song to sing to their kindergarteners who were celebrating birthdays. They couldn't find one, so they wrote their own. They adapted the song "Good Morning to You" to their new "Happy Birthday to You." Sales on the famous birthday song, even after all these years, continue to bring in annual royalties in the hundreds of thousands of dollars.

Sometimes people don't think of adaptation as creative. In fact, some people have told me they consider it stealing. "All he did was take that other person's work and change it!" they protest.

This misconception comes from a misunderstanding of how creativity works. Ideas constantly come from other ideas. An adaptation is truly a new thing. In fact, ideas that aren't adapted come along only once in every thousand years. People who come up with such ideas become known as the super-minds: da Vinci, Newton, Einstein. All others are adapters, including the Aristotles, Emersons, Edisons, Wrights, and the fantastic thinkers who developed the computer chip!

Who can say that Aristotle or Edison *weren't* creative? No one—because they were excellent adapters. And adaptation is a very effective approach to creativity.

Things Parents Can Do

When a child has a problem, parents can help him understand that adaptation is one good way of finding a solution. And

when he uses adaptation naturally, as most of us do, they can point out that he's doing something creative.

One father likes to do experiments with his child to show him adaptation at work. He gives the girl a balloon and asks her to see how many things she can make or do with it. She naturally uses the idea of adaptation to solve the problem.

She may:

1. blow it up and let it fly
2. blow it up and twist it into animals
3. blow it up and write messages on it
4. insert prizes or messages inside before blowing it up
5. rub it on her hair and stick it to the wall

Next time you're in a clothing store, you may want to show your grade schooler how each piece of clothing is merely an adaptation of other types of clothing. A simple blouse is adapted by buttons, sashes, laces, frills, and other trim, as well as by different colors.

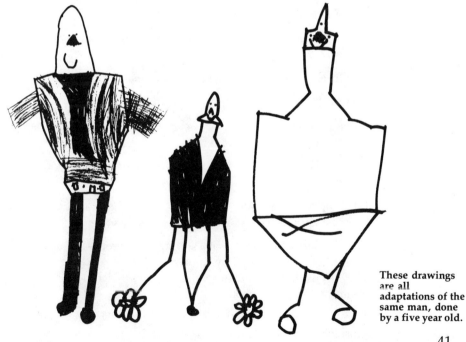

These drawings are all adaptations of the same man, done by a five year old.

Positive Approach

It's much easier to be negative, to find fault, or to criticize than to be positive. It is very hard to be a positive person in our analytical society where the typical point-of-view is negative and downgrading.

Yet the positive is essential to creativity. **Creative thinking is based on looking at things from a positive point of view.** The negative approach critiques or judges what already exists. The positive creative approach seeks to improve, modify, expand, or in some other way come up with a new solution.

When looking at a problem, instead of thinking "This doesn't work," think "How can I improve this?" "How can I change it for the better?" "What can I do to make this work?"

For example, if the food isn't good, ask what will make it better.

If you are unhappy today, ask yourself how you can become happier.

If toys are scattered all over the house, how can you improve the situation?

If the children are upset, what can you do to make them happier?

If your room is a mess, how can you improve it?

If the baby is crying, what can you do to help?

If you are always washing filthy clothes, how can you get the children to keep them cleaner?

If a friend gets mad at you, how can you accept the situation in a positive way?

I like the following story of two kids, one who took the negative approach and one who took the positive:

The first kid was a pessimist. Nothing his parents did could please him. But finally they came up with a perfect idea. They'd give him a whole room full of toys. Then he'd have *nothing* to complain about.

They spent several months shopping on the sly. Then one morning they sprung the surprise on him. They took him to the room and opened the door. It was so full of toys that some fell out onto the floor in front of them.

He took one look at the toys and whined, "Oh, why does there have to be so many? I can't choose. I've seen all these toys before. Why couldn't you get me something new? They'll all get broken anyway."

The other kid was an optimist. He always took the positive approach. He was thrilled with anything his parents did for him. One day they decided to "cure" him—he was just too darned optimistic! So they filled a room with manure. In the morning they took him to the door and started to open it. "We wanted to buy you this special present," they said.

He took one look at the manure and jumped into it, digging for all he was worth. Manure flew every which way. "There's got to be a horse in here somewhere!" he shouted.

Things Parents Can Do

There's an old saying that "any jackass can kick a house down, but it takes a carpenter to build one." Parents can help a child be a carpenter in his life by having a positive approach in their own lives. It's often tough, but a parent should try to be positive in his or her own outlook, should act instead of react. A child will see that approach to life and will seek to copy it. The result will be more creative kids—and a more creative parent!

Experience teaches that parents should be less critical of their children and their actions. This is not easy—it takes hard work. And more hard work. But it's well worth the effort. It helps creativity immensely.

Jackasses are good for kicking houses down. But it takes someone creative to build.

A Sense of Destiny

Jeff liked to draw very early in his life. Even before he started school he enjoyed making pictures of the things around him: his house, his dad, their dog.

As Jeff progressed through school, he didn't lose his desire to draw. In fact, he continued at it, until by the time he was in high school, he acted almost driven about his drawing. While his friends were out playing football in the park, Jeff would be out there sketching the action. When the family went to the ocean for vacation, Jeff sat on the beach and drew the girls.

Jeff's not alone in the world. Generally speaking, **creative people feel they have a destiny that drives them to create**. They almost feel that they don't have a choice in the matter. Something—be it god, devil, muse, or fate—is pushing them in the direction of their creation.

I have a good friend who is pushed in that way to write. He's had several adult jobs in his life, but always he returns to his writing. He can't really explain it, but he can't escape it. He says it's like a "monkey on my back who won't let go. If I keep busy writing, the monkey will let me be. But if I try to sluff, he starts jumping up and down and causing such a racket that soon I have to get back to work."

"Without wishing to be overly dramatic in this matter," psychologist Frank Barron said, "I believe it is literally true that creative individual[s] are willing to stake [their] lives on the meaning of [their] work." How could this be? There's only one answer. Creativity expert Donald MacKinnon says it's the creative person's "sense of destiny."

Things Parents Can Do

Not all people have a sense of destiny—only the most highly creative ones. So not all children will have that monkey on their backs. But if yours does, watch out. Try to understand the child. Be careful not to criticize your child or try to push him away from his creative work. His feelings might be so deeply seated that criticism will only alienate him from you. And his behavior probably won't change.

Learn to Question

How come grass grows skinny leaves and the trees grow fat leaves?

How does water get into the tap?

How come tomatoes grow above the ground and carrots underneath?

Why do birds fly?

Oo-gah-doo-gah-do?

Why are our walls up and down?

What makes a refrigerator work?
How come wheels go around?
Why is our telephone yellow?
Why do dogs bark?

Kids can drive you crazy with their questions. But questioning is an essential part of creativity.

Proper questioning is a key to creative learning. The more limiting the question asked, the less creative the answer or solution will be. The worst kinds of questions, when it comes to creativity, are those that can be answered with a yes or no. But don't worry. Most questions kids ask are more open-ended.

Different kinds of questions and different ways of asking questions are important keys to creativity. It helps to look at the obvious: What is that and why is it that way? Or to question the obvious: Is that really what it looks like? Children who ask those questions (and they all do, until we train it out of them) grow quickly both intellectually and creatively.

Things Parents Can Do

- Answer their children's questions in the best way they can. If they don't know the answers, they can research to find out.

- Encourage questions from children. Too often parents discourage further questioning by the tone of voice they use when they answer the questions.

- Ask questions of their own. Show the child that they value inquisitiveness. Make questions open-ended, not just yes-no. When asking a question of a child, wait for answers, even if it takes several minutes. Let the child think things through if she needs to.

- Show respect for a child's questions. Parents shouldn't ridicule or make fun of them, even when they are way out or when the answers seem obvious. *Obviously* the answer won't be obvious to the child—otherwise he wouldn't ask.

- Finally, they shouldn't laugh if the answer comes out "funny" to them. One father asked his daughter what kind of horse she would like to ride. She said a "whisky" horse (meaning frisky)—and everyone laughed. As a result, she was embarrassed when she needn't have been. This kind of negative feedback causes some children to refrain from asking questions for fear of ridicule.

Division and Omission

David and Brad made some Kool-Aid for the family for April Fool's Day.

"Thanks, boys," said Dad.

"It really looks good," said Mom.

Both boys grinned.

Mom and Dad each took a big swallow from their glasses.

Dad sputtered and coughed. "What is this?" he croaked.

Mom choked and pulled a face.

"April Fool's!" shouted the boys. They had omitted the sugar.

By using the concept of *omission* the boys had come up with a creative way of playing an April Fool's joke on their parents. **Dividing and omitting are both excellent ways to form new creative solutions.** They take existing things or ideas and create totally new ones.

By omitting detail, the artist is able to create a variety of art styles. The eye on the left shows more and more detail omitted. The dot eye at the bottom is used in cartoon characters. Omission enables the artist to express a broad spectrum of creative thoughts.

One mother was having difficulty with her youngest daughter. She wouldn't give up her blanket. The days and weeks passed and the blanket got grungier and grungier. Finally the mom came up with a creative solution by using the idea of division: she cut the blanket in half and washed one half while the child kept the other half in hand. Then she traded to wash the other half.

Foods have been improved through the concept of omission—some meats are made boneless, string beans are grown without the strings, and so forth.

The tubeless tire was created by dividing the traditional tire into two parts—the tire and the tube—and then eliminating the tube part. Spare tires are now being omitted from the car by including instead a new substance that makes tires puncture-proof.

Things Parents Can Do

The best thing parents can do with the idea of division and omission is simply to recognize that the concept exists. They can use it in their own lives, and point it out when their children use it. Through practice the children will come to see the value of the approach and begin to use it more and more.

Small Rewards Can Cause Creativity

"Jimmy, Grandma is coming to visit at two o'clock this afternoon," said Mom. "If you'll draw a nice picture of her by then, I'll give you that $10 you need for Cub Scouts."

Jimmy took out his paper, pencils, and crayons. He looked at the paper. He picked up a pencil, then put it down. He picked up a brown crayon and made a mark. Then he put it down. He pushed the paper away and sat back in his chair. He drew it closer and made another mark. But he just couldn't do it. When Grandma came, all he had was a pile of wadded-up papers.

Mother had imposed too great a task on Jimmy. She had promised him $10, which was a fortune to the boy. **The promise of a reward can increase creativity only if that reward is small. Too large a reward causes a person to become afraid of failure and creativity decreases.**

At one school a number of students were asked to make a simple electric circuit. They were given all the materials and tools they needed—but they were shorted some wire so they'd have to creatively complete the circuit with their screwdriver. Some of the students were offered $25 to do the task, but others were only challenged. Who finished the job? The overwhelming majority was those who were simply challenged. The students who were offered $25 became so anxious over the prospects of getting the money that it interfered with their creativity.

Things Parents Can Do

If you want to give your children rewards for their creativity, keep them small: "When you find five new ways to use popsicle sticks to make something, I've got a surprise for you." The surprise should be something small, perhaps an item of food.

Let the child create at his own speed—and have the reward waiting when he is through.

Need Fosters Creativity

Paul and John wanted to have a jump for their bikes. Paul went in to the garage and got one of his dad's tires. John went into his garage and got a length of board. Paul positioned the tire at the edge of the lawn and John put the board up to it. "Watch me!" John yelled. He rode his bike along the sidewalk as fast as he could up the board, over the tire, and out onto the lawn. "Now it's my turn," said Paul, as he and his bike took off.

But before he hit the jump his dad came out. "Hey! What's going on here? Look what you're doing to the lawn!" But Paul was going too fast to stop. He hit the jump and zoomed out over the grass. Then he skidded to a stop. "All right!" his dad said. "That's it! You're grounded for a week for ruining the lawn."

John and Paul were only doing what the old adage says: Necessity is the mother of invention. They needed a jump for their bikes, and invented one. **When faced with necessity, creativity becomes much easier.** If it is *necessary* to find a creative solution, creativity will increase. The necessity must come from within, however. It just doesn't work to try to force creativity from outside.

Need has caused many creative things to happen. Sir Isaac Newton observed many things in the natural world that confused and intrigued him. Out of his *need* to understand the order of the universe he was able to develop the theory of gravity. Artificial organs were invented because of the *need* to help injured, sick, and/or dying people.

Things Parents Can Do

Remember that children don't have the tools or facilities to meet all their needs, so they become creative. They use boxes for trains and trucks and cars. They use inner tubes from trucks and cars (blown up) to become trampolines. They use spoons for shovels.

Plain blocks (made from 2 x 4's) can be used for most anything, from rooms to roads to vehicles to buildings, etc., whatever the child needs. Keep these types of things around and encourage their use.

When a child asks, "What do you have for . . ." help him see how to improvise. Besides the items just mentioned, good materials to have on hand include string, tape, popsicle sticks, twist ties, a variety of small boards, and so forth.

"Need is the mother of invention."

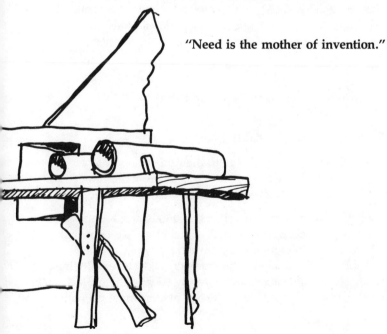

"Necessity is the mother of invention." If a child thinks he needs to build an airplane, he'll find a way.

The Real Solution

Mike was having real problems in school. That was the problem. But the solution was a little more difficult to find. He was tested and then put in a special class for slow learners. He'd been there only a short time when he showed tremendous improvement. So the teacher retested him—and found he *wasn't* slow; he was quite bright.

They returned him to the regular classroom. But his grades dropped again. More tests. This time they learned that Mike had a special hearing problem. Knowing the real problem preceded finding the real solution.

Many solutions to a particular problem may present themselves. Unfortunately, there are usually only one or two *best* solutions. **Only when you find the truly best solution to a problem can you work on it creatively.**

Dr. Walter Reed found the cure to yellow fever by going to the real solution. He spent countless hours trying to find the cause with a microscope. It got him nowhere. Then he attacked it from another angle. He began to study how a man who had not been near anyone with the disease could have gotten it. That led him to the idea of carriers—which led him straight to the mosquito.

Identifying the real solution out of several available ones is one of the things creative people do constantly.

Things Parents Can Do

Allow children to look for more than one solution to a problem. Encourage them to look in a different direction when one solution fails or doesn't work as well as expected.

One effective problem-solving technique is to have children divide their problems into small segments. They then find solutions to each segment, rather than the whole problem. For example, Dr. Reed divided his study of yellow fever into three areas, contacting, cause, and cure. By solving the contact portion of the problem he was soon able to come up with a cure.

Complex or Simple?

The University of California at Berkeley did a study of creative people. The researchers found that **creative people like things to be complex rather than simple.**

That's the good news. It's also the bad.

Preferring things to be complex is good because it brings a richness of experience the person wouldn't otherwise have. It gives him a broader creativity.

But don't forget the bad side. A preference for complexity can tangle up the thoughts. It can mess up the mind to the point that the person never gets to the solutions to his problems, he never produces his creative ideas in the real world.

Complexity manifests itself in other ways. The creative individual's personal life is often full of turmoil and complications such as alcohol, drugs, divorce, and so forth. Because he is unable to see anything in simple terms, the creator often finds his life full of problems and dramatic complexities. It need not be this way, though, if parents will help a creative child simplify things.

Things Parents Can Do

If your child seems to prefer the complex to the simple, watch out. He's probably a creative one. That's good, because creativity is what you want. But it's bad, because of the problems complexity can bring if you don't help the child learn to simplify.

Which drawing do you prefer, the complex one or the simple one? If you like the complex one more, you're more likely to be creative.

Divergent Thinking

Drip, drip, drip. Dad woke suddenly in the middle of the night. Drip, drip, drip. What was making the sound? He checked all the water taps in the house and couldn't find the leak. He listened intently, traced the sound to his son's room. He switched on the light. There on the dresser was a bottle, which was oozing out a green slime. The slime had made its way to the edge of the dresser and was dripping onto the floor—drip, drip, drip.

"Billy!" Dad shook the boy awake. "Look at this mess! Now get up and clean it up this minute!"

What in the world was it? Mom had made Billy some salt-dough to mold things from. She was trying to help him be more creative. Rather than use the dough for molding, Billy had decided to seal it in a bottle to see what would happen. It fermented. And blew the lid off the bottle. Now it was dripping down the side of the bottle and onto the floor.

Billy was using divergent thinking. **Divergent thinking (the opposite of convergent thinking) is the ability to fan out in all directions from an idea.** The initial idea was to play with dough. Billy took it from there.

Brainstorming is an example of divergent thinking: many thoughts grow from a single starting point. Sometimes divergent thoughts are weird and offbeat; and they are always different. It is a non-judgmental type of thinking.

When leaves fall in the autumn, most children pile them up and jump in them. But some children take the leaves and form outlines of rooms, roads, or other things. Children are more apt to divert from the standard type of thinking and doing because they are not locked-in as adults are. To them a screwdriver is not just for driving in screws, but it's a tool for all kinds of things. It can pry, dig, poke, drill, or whatever.

Things Parents Can Do

The ability to think divergently can improve through practice. You can help your child improve his ability by recognizing it when he thinks divergently. Point it out.

One mother likes to take a common object like a file or a spoon and make a game out of how many different uses her children can think of for that object. She asks her child to imagine what uses a common object would have 100 years in the future—or how it may have been used 200 years ago.

How many different things can you cause the box below to become. Look at the variety of things depicted by the box illustrations done. Divergent thinking was used to find the expanded view of the box.

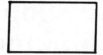

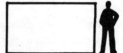

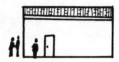

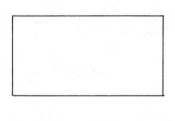

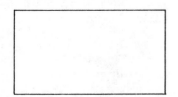

Develop Holistic Thinking

Becky was concocting a cake in the kitchen. She was going to surprise her family with a special treat for supper. But when she started looking for the eggs, she discovered they were out.

She was about to give up on the whole project when she decided to try looking at the problem in its context, to look at it holistically. "Why do I need eggs?" she thought. "Do they give flavor to the cake, or do they do something else?" She did a little quick research in her mom's cookbook and discovered that the eggs were in the cake to help it rise. Then she discovered that mayonnaise is full of eggs and is a good substitute for them.

By thinking holistically, Becky was able to solve her problem. The problem wasn't that she didn't have eggs. It was that she needed something to make the cake rise. And she already had that something—mayonnaise—on hand!

To get good ideas, one must eliminate the imaginary walls that divide the problem up into categories. **The more a person is able to see the "whole" of things, the more he'll be able to discover creative solutions.** Seeing the whole means seeing how all things relate to one another in some way.

Sir Isaac Newton was able to change the whole course of physics by thinking holistically, by making a connection between a falling apple and the bodies in the heavens. William Harvey made a major contribution to modern medicine by making a connection between the functioning of a pump and the working of the human heart.

Things Parents Can Do

Try imagining how things might relate to other things. What do apples have in common with concrete? Why must worms squirm?

It's fun for children to try to see similarities or relationships between various elements in their surroundings. Encourage them to see the "whole" of things.

Trading One for Another

Our present car windshield wipers came about through substitution. The first windshield wipers were operated by hand. Then in 1912 John Oishei substituted forced air for the hand; he used air pressure from the air intake of the engine to operate the wipers. Later, when the engine was used to produce electricity, as in our modern car, the electricity was substituted for the forced air to power the wipers.

A lot of problems with clothing have been solved through creative substitution. Through substitution of synthetic fibers for natural ones, researchers have been able to make clothing wrinkle-proof, stain-resistant, fire-resistant, lighter, tougher, cheaper, and more long-lasting.

Substitution is a great approach to creativity. **When a person substitutes a new part, idea, or solution for another, he or she is being creative.**

Janalee lost her first tooth—and was she ever excited! She knew that if she put the tooth under her pillow that night she'd get some money back from the tooth fairy. The next morning, first thing, she groped under her pillow. Sure enough! A quarter.

"I ran out of lemonade, so I found some other yellow stuff."

That afternoon while playing in the back yard she noticed some white berries on a bush. They were all dried out, small and hard—just like her tooth.

She took one of the berries and put it under her pillow that night, thinking that now she had a real good source for additional money.

But when she reached under her pillow the next morning, she didn't find any money—only a small note. It said, "You can't fool the tooth fairy!"

Janalee had used substitution as a creative way to get money, substituting the berry for a tooth. But the tooth fairy had also used substitution, putting a note under the pillow instead of money!

Children are very good at substitution. Their brains aren't all locked up like ours often are. When one child was told he couldn't use matches to start fires, he substituted: he found a magnifying glass and used that. In another home, the children were told not to TOUCH the cookies on the table. Determined to obey, they still found a creative way to get to the cookies. They substituted pencils for their fingers, picking up the cookies and putting them into their mouths without TOUCHING them. All they did was eat them.

One teenaged boy, as punishment for a wrongdoing, was told he couldn't drive the family car for a week. So he substituted: he drove his girlfriend's car. He took his punishment, but through creativity was able to make it so it didn't hurt too much.

Things Parents Can Do

Understand what substitution is.

Recognize when your children use substitution.

Don't punish your children when they use substitution. They are being strictly honest and are taking you at your literal word. Instead, help them to understand what they're doing. The more your child realizes the value of substitution, the more he'll be able to use it as a creative tool.

Dreams

Robbie hopped out of bed and padded into his parents' bedroom. "Mommy, Mommy!" he whispered. "I just had a beautiful dream."

His mommy grunted and he continued. "We were all swimming at the pool and these lights came out of the sky. They dropped down toward us. We stopped swimming and just looked at them. They came closer and closer—they were all beautiful, bright and with lots of colors. Then, when they got right above us, they started dancing. It was like angels dancing in the sky. I wanted to watch them forever, but I woke up."

Mommy grunted again.

"Well, 'night, Mommy. Maybe I can dream that again." And he was off to bed.

Dreams are a real storehouse of creative ideas. The person who can remember and utilize his dreams will be more creative than the person who forgets all about them.

Thomas Edison is famous for his midday catnaps. He'd sleep only a few hours at night, then would get the rest of his sleep in catnaps during the day. One reason for that approach was his reliance on dreams for ideas. Whenever he was stumped by a problem, he'd stretch out in his Menlo Park workshop, and, half-dozing, get an idea that would help him.

See that sweet little kid sleeping peacefully in his room? It could well be that he's developing some of the most creative solutions of his life.

Acclaimed science fiction writer Ray Bradbury uses a similar approach for getting ideas. "Quite often I do discover some preciously good material in the half-awakened, half-slumbery time before real sleep. Quite often I have forced myself completely awake to make notes on ideas thus come upon," he says.

Nightmares can also be useful. Inventor Elias Howe had spent years trying to develop his sewing machine—and he was failing. Then one night he dreamed that if he didn't invent the machine within twenty-four hours, cannibals would eat him. In the dream he failed to meet the deadline—and the cannibals descended, wielding sharp spears. In the tip of each spear was a hole. Howe awakened, sweating. And then he realized he had his solution: he would put a hole in the bottom end of the needle, just like the spears!

Things Parents Can Do

We usually think dreams just come out of the blue, but they *can* be prompted. You can give your child a real boost by teaching him the process whereby *he* can have creative dreams:

1. Put a pad and pencil by the bed.
2. Before going to sleep, go over the problem in your mind.
3. Tell yourself to dream about the problem—and to awaken just after the dream.
4. Go to sleep.
5. Wake up and review the dream, with your eyes still closed. (Opening the eyes will bring in visual input that may confuse the mind.)
6. Quickly write down the key points of what you dreamed—even if it seems like nonsense.
7. Go back to sleep.

In the morning go over your notes and fill in the details.

Pursue the creative thought during the day. Eventually you'll determine if it's helpful and usable or if it should simply be discarded. If you need more help, repeat this whole process.

Mother Nature and a Good Idea

Ferde Grofe was so impressed with the splendid magnificence of the Grand Canyon that he wrote a series of short musical pieces describing it, his famous *Grand Canyon Suite*. In the suite, Grofe uses the different sounds and melodies of his music to express his feelings about the high walls and deep valleys of the canyon; he describes the sky, the clouds, the storm, the donkeys walking down into the canyon, the flowers by the side of the trail.

Grofe's love of nature caused him to write his Grand Canyon Suite. The natural beauty of the Grand Canyon inspired him and gave him the sounds and feelings he tried to recreate in his musical piece.

Nature can be the source of many of our creative solutions. The more a child learns about the world around him, the more creative he'll be able to be.

Lisa squatted on the patio and looked at the fuzzy creature crawling by her feet. "Look, mommy. It's a fat, fuzzy worm!"

Her mom looked up from her book. "Hey, it's a caterpillar! Pick it up gently and you'll feel it's funny feet on your hand."

"You can observe a lot just by watching."
—Yogi Berra

Lisa gingerly picked the caterpillar up and let it crawl up her arm. She smiled broadly. "It tickles," she said. "It's funny!"

Children have a natural attraction to nature. They like the plants and the animals and the bugs. They like to explore. They like to learn about the world around them. That's a good trait to have when it comes to creativity.

Examples of creative solutions from nature are legion:

Velcro was fashioned after the stickery burdock burr.

Radar is patterned after the bats sonar radar system which enables him to fly through darkness without running into objects.

Modern automatic-focus cameras were designed to work like the human eye.

The idea of military camouflage was adopted after learning from all sorts of animals in their natural habitat. The preying mantis changes colors according to whether he's on a green leaf or a brown twig. From the preying mantis, military experts got the creative idea to make soldiers' clothing a mixture of green and brown, to help them blend into forest and jungle backgrounds better. Tanks and trucks are also painted green and brown.

The hypodermic needle came into being when researchers copied the rattlesnake's fangs. The fangs pierce the skin and the rattlesnake venom shoots through the fangs hollow center into the victim.

Submarines use the same principle for underwater ballast as a fish's bladder.

A firefly is 80 percent more efficient than our incandescent lamps. Using what they learned from the firefly, scientists have developed an efficient chemical flashlight.

Things Parents Can Do

Enjoy nature with your children. Show them how insects use camouflage, how their legs bend, how their eyes work. Show them how leaves turn with the sun—and how they won't grow green if they aren't in the sunlight. The more familiar your child can become with the world around him, the more data he'll have stored in his brain to use creatively.

Order and Tradition

Fred is a stuffy kid. His parents have carefully reared him to act "properly". Emily Post is his idol. Fred's most creative move—for which he was quickly reprimanded—was to change the position of the silverware at his place setting at the table.

Marcy lives in a museum. At least that's what it feels like. She can hardly touch the furniture. She's not allowed to decorate her room. Playing with "messy" things like glue and playdough are discouraged. Her mom has a constant refrain: "Marcy, don't make a mess. We want to keep the house neat and clean."

Stan's parents are very tied to tradition. They feel good about the past, and they want to retain firm ties with what has gone before. Whenever Stan wants to start a project, something new to him, his mom or dad is right there beside him. "Here's how you do this. Here's how we've always done this. Here's how we did this when we were kids."

Order and tradition have their place in our lives. It's nice to have a clean, orderly house. It's stabilizing to have a grip on our past and to establish certain habit patterns in our lives.

But when order and tradition become dominant concerns, creativity goes out the window. **The more orderly and traditional the approach, the less innovative the person will be.**

Children need to be free to make messes. They need to be free to do things their own way. Only by experimenting and feeling their own way through a problem will they learn. Only then will they develop the creative skills that are so essential in life.

Texas millionaire Stanley Marsh gives us a good example of approaches that disregard order and tradition. He wanted to have some nice landscaping elements along his driveway—but he wasn't really excited about having ornamental rocks or shrubs. So he started looking around. He had always been intrigued at the design of the tailfins of 1950s Cadillacs. As he thought about it, he decided, "Hey, what the heck!"

Stanley Marsh bought a batch of old Cadillacs and buried them headfirst along his driveway, with the fins sticking out.

Another example: once he found someone else using his reserved parking space, even though it was clearly marked. And Stanley needed it! But rather than call a tow truck, he disregarded order and tradition and had the offending car welded to a light pole.

I'm not suggesting we all go around burying cars in the ground or welding cars to poles. Only millionaires get to do those things!

But we can all free our thinking from order and tradition. If we do, we'll end up being more creative. And the parents who encourage (and allow) their children to form new patterns of thinking end up with more creative children.

Things Parents Can Do

First, a parent should try to differentiate between creating and misbehaving. A child might act the way he does because he's seeking to learn, or he's seeking to solve a problem—not because he's "naughty." Allow him the freedom to explore and to make mistakes.

It's helpful to have the attitude that a clean house is sometimes not as important as a creative child. (Now how many mothers will use this as an excuse not to clean the house?)

Realize, too, that the traditional way of doing something may not be the best way for your child. It may be more important for him to work through something *creatively* than it is to work through it *quickly and efficiently*. Only you can be the judge of that.

Turning Things Around

Light fixtures were reversed to come up with a creative new way of lighting a room. They were designed to shine up rather than down, giving us the reflected light that is so popular today.

Lately indoor tennis courts have been putting this idea to good use. Reflected light is much better to play tennis in, since it gives more even illumination. But in the past indoor tennis courts have been illuminated by direct lighting. The shadow effect caused by direct lights was a real drawback to the courts.

Then someone came up with a good solution to the problem. The answer was creative, though simple: reverse the lights. Point them up, instead of down; have the lighting reflected down, rather that shining directly down.

"I flew in from New York today. Boy, are my arms tired!"

Creative solutions are often achieved simply by reversing things. When a creative person is stumped, he can sometimes find the answer to his problem by turning the situation around, looking at the backside, turning things bottom up.

Comedians use this approach to come up with creative new jokes. Instead of the dog biting the man, they tell of the man biting the dog.

Life magazine once reported how Dale Carson, a new sheriff in Duval County, Florida, creatively used the approach of reversal:

"He noticed something that other sheriffs, over the ages, had failed to see: the bread and water treatment usually doesn't work. He discovered that young toughs gloried in being so punished because it proved how tough they were and they could brag about the bread and water treatment when they got out.

"So, ingeniously, Sheriff Carson substituted baby food for bread and water. Now the glory-seekers get strained beef, carrots, beef liver, spinach and applesauce. They eat it because they're hungry but they don't brag about it.

" 'It's no fun,' says Carson, 'to tell your buddies you were so tough they had to put you on baby food. One day usually gets them on their best behavior.' "

65

A golfer named Vash Young solved a problem in a similar way. Young was concerned with the profanity golfers were using on the course. He felt it was a bad influence on the caddies and younger people out golfing.

But how to solve it was a real challenge. Young knew that he couldn't just ask the golfers to quit. They'd just laugh at him.

Then he thought of a way to a creative solution through reversal. He hung a sign up by the cash register that said, half-humorously: "All golfers are hereby ordered to utter a coarse swear-word every time they miss a shot. Since your young caddy is at a very impressionable age, this should be done in near proximity of him so he can get the full benefit of this kind of behavior."

The proclamation had amazing results. The golfers cleaned up their language from the very first day—all through reversal.

Things Parents Can Do

We've all heard of reverse psychology. Tell the child to do things you *don't* want him to do—and through pigheadedness he'll refuse. In the end you get just what you wanted.

That's an example of reversal. You can use that approach on your kids, and sometimes it will work. If your child is being a poop, tell him you want him to be crabby or pouty that day. You'll probably get the opposite result.

The next day you can reveal one of your trade secrets and help him understand reversal better.

It may also be helpful to point out to your child times when he's using reversal on his own. The more he understands the basic idea of reversal, the more he'll be able to use it consciously in his own problem solving.

A simple reversal will turn this frown into a smile.

Games and Puzzles

How can games and puzzles promote creativity? After all, when you play them you're only following rules. You're not coming up with new solutions, new ideas, or anything different at all. It's true that not all games and puzzles are creative, but **mind-expanding games and puzzles can promote creativity and the imagination.**

Some of these include:
charades, role playing, imitating animals, etc.
chess
sports—basketball, football, etc. (particularly if you seek creative team strategy)
hunting and fishing
puzzle solving
crossword puzzles
riddles
guessing games
building blocks—legos, lincoln logs, etc. (One father went to where a construction company was building several new homes. He got permission to gather up all the 2x4 end pieces. He took these home, sanded and varnished them, and gave them to his boys for Christmas. The sizes ranged from very small to fairly large. The two boys played with these blocks in many different ways clear into their teens.)
sandpiles
jingles—riding, jumping rope, etc.
puppets (both making and playing with them). Puppets can be made with salt dough, then painted. Clothes can be made for them. Or make them from paper bags.

One easy way to make a puzzle is to get a picture from a magazine, cut it up, and then put it back together again.

Adding To

Rick had a new motocross dirt bike he loved to ride and race, but he couldn't afford the pads to go on the handlebars or crossbar.

One day his father bought some insulation for the pipes connected to the water heater. Before they could be put on the pipes, two pieces "appeared" on Paul's bike. They made inexpensive pads which became the envy of all Rick's friends.

"Adding to" is a method of creativity often used unconsciously. If it were used consciously more often a child's creative abilities would grow. "Adding to" includes making things bigger, stronger, or more valuable. It involves adding more parts or more ingredients. **Adding to existing things is a way to form new creative solutions.**

Narrow auto tires used to have problems with ruts in the roads, resulting in rough rides. So tire manufacturers "added to," making the tires fatter—the balloon tire of today. These in turn are being made fatter still for racing or for style.

Shatterproof glass is made by sandwiching a plastic sheet between layers of glass. Toothpaste was improved by adding flouride to prevent cavities. Contact lenses are additions which improve sight.

The environment is improved by "adding to." Music soothes when added. Lighting enhances, softens, brightens, or highlights room environments, depending on how it is added. Pictures, mirrors, plants, and other items can be added to further change the environment.

Things Parents Can Do

"Adding to" is a helpful creative approach—but a child can use it more effectively if he knows about it. When your child creates by "adding to," you can call his attention to what he's done. Gradually he'll add that to his repertoire of conscious creative approaches.

"Great Job!"

What if your child had done this drawing? What would you say to encourage him to further develop his creativity?

"No stimulus to creative effort is so effective as a good pat on the back," says Ernest Benger of DuPont. "Do anything to encourage . . . ideas."

Hotel magnate E. M. Statler told of an experience he had while he was a young bellboy in the early 1900s. He realized that hotel guests hesitated to call for ice water because the bellboys had to tote pitchers up long flights of stairs. As he considered the problem, he got the idea of piping water up to the rooms.

That taught him something about ideas—and encouraging them. "I never fail to realize that some bellboy of mine could dish up just as good an idea as that," he said. Because of that attitude he always gave out rewards for good ideas—and as a result, employees were much more willing to bring ideas to him. His business prospered as it otherwise couldn't have.

If you give your child these kinds of encouragement, he'll want to do more drawing in the future. **Encouragement cultivates creativity.** And the more encouragement there is, the more the child will want to create.

This is especially true if the encouragement comes from someone the child really cares about. When you're young, home and family form the center of your universe. Children look to their parents for direction and support. When a parent encourages his child in a particular direction, the child will acknowledge and respond to that encouragement.

People want to do things that make them feel good. Praise and compliments are things that really help a child feel better about himself. When you praise your child for creativity, he'll seek to be creative some more, to win more praise.

Things Parents Can Do

Be sure to compliment or praise your child when he or she does something creative. Be specific. Alex Osborn has said, "Creativity is so delicate a flower that praise tends to make it bloom."

It's a little thing to acknowledge or praise a child's creativity. And even if the creation seems silly or insignificant to the parent, the effort is big and important to the child.

When your child describes a creation he made when you weren't around, listen to him. Don't be like the parent who turns off by acting uninterested or by reading the paper through the child's explanation. For when we fail to encourage, we often end up *dis*couraging. And discouragement is a real creativity killer.

Here are a few ideas to get you thinking:

Never ridicule—Don't say, "What in the world is that?" or "That's not the way to do a cow!"

Be free with praise—"I love the way you draw!" "Your drawings are some of my most favorite in the whole world."

Avoid comparisons—Don't say, "That's not nearly as good as Chucky's drawing." "You can do better than that. Your drawings were better than that last year!"

Look for the good—"You're really learning how to use colors, aren't you." "I really like the way you make your lines nice and dark." "You've put a lot of different shades of lines, haven't you. That's great!"

Be interested—"I like what you've done here. Tell me about it." "What were you feeling when you did this part?"

Be excited—"I'm so glad you showed this to me!" "Can I keep this drawing to hang on the refrigerator?"

Seeing It in Your Mind

"Once upon a time," said Daddy, "a daddy and a boy were walking down the road when they saw a cute brown dog with a black spot on his . . ."

"Foot," said Todd. "The spot was some tar because some men had been fixing the road and the dog stepped in the tar. The dog went up to the daddy and . . ."

"Wagged his tail," continued Dad. "So the daddy reached down to pet the dog when it . . ."

"Ran off into the bushes at the side of the road," said Todd. "So the daddy and the boy went on down the road till they saw a yellow . . ."

Daddy and Todd are being creative through *speculative imagery*. They are visualizing fiction in their minds. With speculative imagery a person can use his imagination to creatively envision things he's never seen before.

Speculative imagery can turn one object into many others—even if that object is yourself!

Speculative imagery is an important creative skill. Creative thinkers, such as Einstein was, are often able to "see" in their minds the things they want to invent or create. Fiction writers and playwrights develop the skill to imagine settings they've never seen—and then place imagined people in those settings.

The more this skill is developed, the more creative a person becomes. Todd is a good example. The more he plays the story game with his dad, the better he gets.

Things Parents Can Do

Some parents tell stories like Dad and Todd do—one person starts, the next continues, the first tells some more, and so on.

Or they read the first part of a short story and let the child make up an ending.

Some try reading to their children stories that don't have exact details of settings, then the children are asked to explain the details as they've visualized them.

They'll listen with their children to the old radio plays that are now being rebroadcast. These provide rich opportunities for imaginative visualization.

They'll have their children make up stories about pictures they show to them.

Beware of TV! It's a real killer when it comes to speculative imagination. It doesn't leave visual gaps for kids to fill in.

Hard Work

How do you get a child to clean his room?
Hang up his clothes?
Mow the lawn?
Pull the weeds?
Wash and/or dry the dishes?
Sweep the floor?
Put away his toys?
Put away tools or utensils used?

These are problems all parents face: How do you get a child to work? The issue extends beyond getting chores done. Even more important is that the child learn *how* to work. The child who learns how to work hard and for long periods of time is the one most likely to be creative. Because **creative people work hard and for long hours.**

Throughout history the most creative people were those who were diligent workers, who didn't give up when they were tired and worn out. Often their most creative solutions came when they had pushed nearly to the point of exhaustion.

Thomas Edison was the owner of 1,093 patents when he died. Some of those came easy—but many did not. Edison was so committed to hard work that he trained himself to get by on only a few hours sleep each night. "Genius is ten percent inspiration and ninety percent perspiration," he said.

Henry Ford had to work years before he was able to produce a commercially successful car. He was so committed to his work that he often spent all night in his shop—after working all day for Edison's company!

Alexander Graham Bell invented the telephone when he was quite young. He could have sat back on his laurels and collected good money from his invention. But he was a creative person, and he was driven to hard work.

All through Bell's life he pushed himself to try to come up with another outstanding creation like the telephone. He didn't want to go to the grave with the feeling that he'd made only one contribution to society, however important. And he didn't want to die thinking the last years of his life had no value.

One of the last things Bell developed was the transmission of sound by light waves. That method of transmission is now proving to be even better than the electronic means that have been used in telephones up till now. Many of the new phone systems are going to fiber optics, incorporating his ideas.

His capacity for hard work appears to have paid off: his last invention may prove to be one of his greatest.

Ask any writer about his "muse." He'll tell you he'd love to get one. But in the meantime he has to plug away, forcing the words out, one after another. He can't wait for the creative spirit to strike. He has to work hard *first*.

Like Edison, many creative people ascribe their success not to uncommon abilities but to plain old hard work.

Things Parents Can Do

The parent who teaches his child to work will be doing him a great favor as far as creativity goes. Here's the sequence every creative person must follow: stirrings of creativity, hard work to develop it, success!

How can a parent teach work? This is something that is a continual challenge to most parents. Some suggested approaches might include:

- Assign each child specific chores, appropriate to his age.
- Begin at an early age to expect the child to be responsible to do his share of the work around the house.
- Attach rewards and punishments to help the child get the chores done. The rewards may be as simple as a word of praise or thanks. But then *don't nag or fuss*. Give out the reward or punishment, as promised.
- Be consistent. Children soon learn if the parent is a pushover.

Accept The Unpredictable

Julie turns her glass of milk over on the table and draws in the milk with her fingers while she is eating dinner.

Timmy mixes his food together in an unappetizing glump and then eats the glump instead of eating the individual foods separately.

Billy tries to suck up his food with a straw instead of using his fork or spoon.

Children often do many unpredictable things. For example, Lori flushed her little sister's diaper down the toilet to see if it would go all the way. (It didn't.) David gave his cat a haircut with the lawn clippers. (Or tried. The cat got away pretty much unscathed. David got away with a nasty batch of scratches.) Susie's mother caught her just as she was putting the puppy in the washing machine to bathe him.

Creative people do the unpredictable. They recognize that they'll make mistakes along the way—and tolerate it. When your children make mistakes—if you want them to develop their creativity—you also need to be tolerant.

Certainly children aren't unique in doing the unpredictable. One man played a joke on his vacationing boss by having all the locks changed at work. Another worker exchanged the sugar for the salt in a fellow worker's lunch pail.

Things Parents Can Do

Since adults often do screwy things for fun and for creativity, they need to accept it and tolerate it in their children. Some of the creative things your children do will drive you nuts—but why am I telling *you*? It helps, though, if you realize the child's behavior is an expression of his creativity, and not misbehavior. The three best things parents can do when a child does unpredictable things as he develops his creativity are:

1. Be tolerant
2. Develop a sense of humor
3. Be tolerant and develop a sense of humor.

Multiple Skills

"All I do is run," a mother complained to her neighbor. "Mary has tap dancing on Monday, swimming on Tuesday, piano on Wednesday, Brownies on Thursday, and gymnastics on Friday. I know I'm supposed to feel liberated nowadays, but I just feel like a chauffeur!"

"Feel lucky," said the other mother. "We've tried to interest Jane in different things, but all she wants to do is watch TV."

It's easy to see which of these two kids is doing more to develop her creativity. Of course a parent doesn't have to go to the extreme that Mary's mom is. But helping your child learn multiple skills is very influential in the development of creativity.

Creative people have traditionally enjoyed a wide variety of skills. Benjamin Franklin, for instance, was proficient as a statesman, soap maker, printer, writer, editor, and gardener. He was also an inventor—bifocals, the Franklin stove, and so forth.

Such people are sometimes called a "jack of all trades" but with creative effort they are able to be masters of them all. People like Ben Franklin teach us an important principle: **Most creative people have several skills.**

Take this little self-test, and you'll see what I mean. Write down the names of five famous entertainers who have multiple skills and list their skills:

1.

2.

3.

4.

5.

How did you do? If you really tried, I'm sure you were able to come up with five—and more. Just consider: Robert Redford was a top box-office name as an actor. Then he decided to go into directing. His first effort, *Ordinary People,* won an Oscar as best picture of the year.

Barbra Streisand was internationally recognized as a singer. Then she decided to try her hand at acting, and immediately became one of the most popular actresses of our time.

Henry Fonda has starred in scores of films. He is also a painter who produces pieces of art that many consider to be outstanding.

Cheryl Ladd became prominent in the popular television series *Charlie's Angels.* But she has also proved quite impressive in TV specials as a singer and dancer.

Mikhail Barishnikov is one of the greatest ballet dancers of all time. But he has also starred in movies that prove he also has creative skill as an actor.

There are a multitude of other examples I could name. I mention these only because their names are familiar to almost everybody.

But if you were to list your own creative abilities, I'd suspect that you'd be able to mention several. Creative people usually have several skills.

"To have only one skill forces you into a narrow approach to the world," said David Campbell. "People who are only good with hammers see every problem as a nail."

Things Parents Can Do

Try to allow your children to develop all the skills they can by letting them play Little League ball, go to summer camp, attend summer school classes, take lessons of all kinds (music, art, skill, crafts, etc.), participate in scouting, 4-H, arts and crafts, etc. Help them to become good at several skills and to have knowledge of several more. The more skills they develop, the more creative they'll be able to be.

Don't Take Things Too Seriously

"Hey, Mom. Listen to the song I made up." Bobby began to pound away on the piano.

After about fifteen seconds his mom had had enough. "That's not a song!" she shouted over the noise. "That's just racket. Now knock it off!"

Bobby's mom was taking things too seriously. Bobby had learned to make new sounds on the piano—and he called them a song. For him it was a new discovery. But his mother would accept it only at its face value: noise!

In some families everything is very serious or intense all the time. Family members don't develop or practice a good sense of humor. Mistakes are not tolerated. And children grow up stiff, stifled, uncreative.

Remember this: Everyone doesn't do every little thing right every time. And when someone wins, someone else loses. In a family, everything shouldn't be serious all the time. Family members need freedom to give and take, a tolerance of mistakes, an ability to see humor in things that happen. When parents tolerate **the ups and down of children's creative efforts, the children's creativity will increase.** Families need to *not* take things seriously all the time.

Things Parents Can Do

Some ideas to consider:
1. Be tolerant of children's mistakes. Don't let these mistakes bug you. Children are imperfect human beings (just as parents are); it's impossible for them to go through life without making mistakes.

2. Have a sense of humor. Enjoy your children's creations, no matter how silly, stupid, or insignificant they are on the surface. Your child pounds on the piano? Tell him you like his song— but "will you please play it a little more softly?"

3. Don't be too literal. When a child is being imaginative, be imaginative with him!

Preconceptions

Children don't often have preconceived notions, but parents do. And they can rub off on the kids.

Don't be misled by preconceived notions. For example, many people tried to improve the broom. They failed.

Then a guy came along and decided to make a whole new invention, to replace the broom. He puttered around and fiddled around—finally he had what he needed. Brooms worked by pushing the dirt away from where you wanted it. Great! His preconceived notions gave him just what was needed: a blowing machine.

He took it to a demonstration. "Look at what I've got here!" he boasted. He turned on the machine and grinned broadly as it blew all the dirt off the stage—right into the audience's faces.

H. G. Booth was sitting in the audience, and he saw the problem right off. Preconceived notions were holding everyone back. The problem wasn't poorly designed brooms; and the answer wasn't copying the broom with an electrical device.

The problem was removing dirt! So Booth threw out the broom and he threw away the blowing machine and invented the vacuum cleaner. Instead of pushing dirt away, he pulled it toward him!

Preconceived notions stifle creativity. They cause us to see only one solution—usually the one that already exists.

Join all the dots by drawing only four lines—without taking your pencil off the paper. It's possible—but only if all preconceived notions are left behind. (See the next page to find out how it's done.)

This optical illusion seems awfully strange because we see it as we "expect" it to appear.

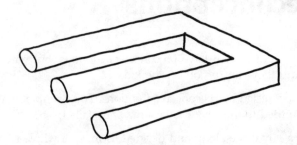

When parents encourage their children to use things differently, those children won't suffer from preconceived notions. One father bought some small fire extinguishers that were on sale. He removed the chemicals inside and filled the extinguishers with water for his kids: giant squirt guns! Outside only, of course!

Another father, not quite so rich, got some free 35cc syringes (without needles) from a horse-raising friend. He cleaned them out good and—yup! More squirt guns. As these fathers broke their own preconceived notions, they were able to free the thinking of their children. That's a key. As a parent lets *herself* be open in her thinking, she also trains her children in openness—and creativity.

Things Parents Can Do

Parents should channel their own thinking so that they are open to new thinking and creative ideas. Then they can help their children do the same thing.

Show them new and different ways to use commonplace items. For example, inner tubes are not used just for inflating tires, but also for trampolines, for floating down streams and on lakes, for tubing down hills on the snow, and for rolling down hills in the summertime.

Answer to problem on previous page: I didn't tell you not to go past the boundaries, but a lot of people don't anyway, because of preconceived notions.

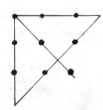

"I Can't!"

How can a kid create positive things when all his thinking is so negative?

"Oh, it won't work anyway."

"I can't do it; I'm not good enough."

"Nothing ever works out very well for me."

"That'll probably be just another mistake."

Self-discouragement. It's a real creativity killer. And everyone of us—especially our children—is subject to it.

Creative individuals often have a real struggle getting their ideas out. They attack things from a different angle than the norm—and others are utterly unable to see their idea until it's clarified or refined. The result is that the creator finds himself going through a period of loneliness and isolation as he polishes and perfects his idea.

And when things don't go well, he's wide open to self-discouragement—and sometimes criticism from others. If he lets it get him down, he may lose his creative drive.

Learning to fight discouragement is one of the primary tasks of the creative person. **Discouragement stifles creativity.** Discouragement is so powerful that it could totally destroy a person's momentum on a given project.

"Which is worse—to look foolish to others, or to look foolish to yourself? Some may think that some of your ideas are half-baked; but what could be sillier than for you to let that stop you from trying to make the most of your mind?"
—Alex Osborne

Things Parents Can Do

Teach your children to have fun creating, to be tolerant of their own mistakes. Tell them, "You've only tried one way. There are a dozen others to try before you quit."

At the same time, show your children you can be tolerant of yourself. When you make mistakes, forgive yourself and keep after the problem.

If you can show your children that you support them, they won't feel so isolated when they're working on a problem. They'll know you're interested and concerned, and they'll have someone to talk things out with.

Try things to "find out what the result will be." Half the fun of creating is to see what will happen.

Modification

"Come see my car," said Bobbie. He was sitting in a box from the grocery store.

"I've got a tunnel," bragged Jimmy. He'd taken the bottom out of his box and was crawling back and forth through it.

"And what are you using your box for?" asked Alena's mother.

Alena looked up and smiled. "Mine is a doll house." She was busy arranging doll furniture and dolls in her box.

Boxes are a good example of how things can be creatively modified. Two eight year olds took three boxes, two paper towel rolls, tape, twine, gray paint, and a mirror and came up with a submarine that they used for several weeks until it wore out. In the book *Christina Katerina and the Box*, by Patricia Gauch, Christina used the same refrigerator box for a castle, a club house, a racing car, and the floor of a ballroom.

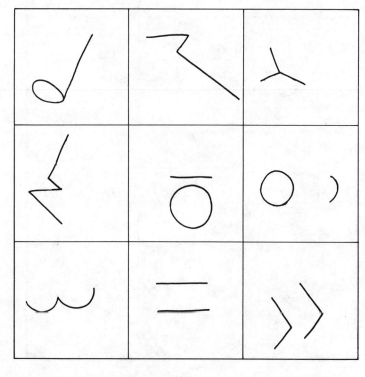

Modify each of these figures to make some kind of picture out of it.

Modification is changing existing things or ideas to form new solutions. It's a very useful creative approach. Louis Pasteur modified the temperature of wine to kill dangerous microbes without spoiling the wine taste. Then he modified the same process to develop the "pasteurization" process that makes milk safe to drink.

The electric light bulb constantly attracted bugs—until it was modified to a yellow color.

In the 1500s, da Vinci invented the roller bearing which was a round cylinder. In 1898, Henry Timkin modified the design by tapering the cylinder. The bearing thus became more usable. The even more usable spherical ball bearing was later modified from Timkin's design.

Things Parents Can Do

When your child is stuck on a problem, suggest ways he can modify existing elements to find a solution. Help him keep the concept in his mind until it's a part of his creative approach.

One person took a good look at the problem on the preceding page and came up with these creative solutions. What were yours like?

Environment Promotes or Kills Creativity

Unfortunately, today's typical environment doesn't go well with creativity. This is especially true of schools, which teach the type of thinking that stifles creativity. For example, the teacher will give all the children the same color paper and tell them to mark, color, and fold it in the same way, and then cut it out in the exact same pattern. If they were given the same color paper and asked to form as many different things as they could with it, then the school would be teaching creativity. But they don't.

You'd think that a college graduate would be more creative than someone without that experience. At least, you'd hope it. "College graduates *should* rate higher than non-college people in creative aptitude," says Alex Osborne. Of course they should. Experience leads to greater potential for creativity. But although they *should*, Osborne concludes that they *don't*. Why? Because their *environment* has trained it out of them.

The setting or situation in which a person finds himself—his environment—can promote creativity. Or kill it.

As we were preparing this book, we got together with six or eight friends to talk about creativity. After we'd discussed ideas for a while, we decided to list all the creative things we'd done while growing up.

That's where the surprise came in. Collectively, we came up with 100 ideas, all different. But, interestingly, 92 of those ideas came from just two of us.

What made the difference? Environment! Both those people had had a stimulating environment while they were growing up.

Then the group started to notice something else: those two people were the ones with the creative kids. Because of their upbringing, they just naturally established homes where their kids could be creative. They kept the atmosphere open and comfortable for their children.

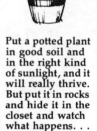

Put a potted plant in good soil and in the right kind of sunlight, and it will really thrive. But put it in rocks and hide it in the closet and watch what happens. . .

Things Parents Can Do

Parents can improve the environment by:

1. Keeping tools available for the child to work with creatively such as Dad's tools and work bench, a separate set of tools for the child, secondhand utensils the child can use as desired.
2. Keep materials for creativity available: fasteners, glue, scissors, paper, wheels, popsicle sticks, rubber bands, crayons, paints, chalk.
3. Buy appropriate toys for creativity: Legos, Erector sets, blocks, Lincoln logs, Tinkertoys, etc.
4. As much as possible, refrain from using TV. This is a passive, not a creative tool. It creates no incentive for creativity.
5. As much as possible, listen to dramatic programs on the radio. This causes the child to participate mentally; it creates images in his mind.

Most important of all, do what you can to establish a creative atmosphere in your home. Be encouraging when your children want to create. Be excited about the creations they show you.

Set up places where they can create.

Set up times when they can create.

Accept fouled up experiences.

Playing Around

Three-year-old Betty was getting restless in the doctor's office. They'd been sitting there *so* long. "How would you like to make a peanut butter sandwich?" asked Mother.

"Yeah. I'm hungry."

"Well, you can't make one to eat—but you can make one out of yourself. First, take off your sandles. Then put peanut butter on this foot." She pointed to Betty's right foot. "Then put jam on this foot." She pointed to Betty's left foot. "Then put the bottoms of both your feet together—and you have a peanut butter sandwich!"

Mother took a pretend knife and spread peanut butter on Betty's right foot and jam on her left foot and then pressed the soles together. Betty giggled and sat holding her "sandwich."

"Who's going to eat it?" Betty asked.

"I will," answered Mommy, and she took a big pretend bite.

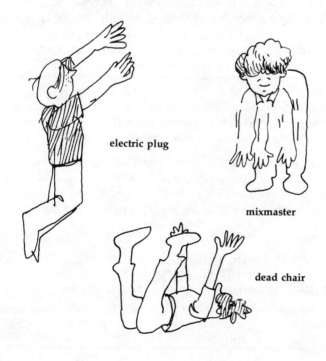

electric plug

mixmaster

dead chair

Playfulness and creativity go hand-in-hand. In fact, often it's impossible to have one without the other. Try playing a game of charades with your children. It is difficult for young children to dramatize things they are unfamiliar with. So have them imitate things around the house.

Four-year-old Danny loved to have daddy make a cake on his tummy. All the ingredients were added, one at a time. And then the cake was mixed (by tickling the tummy). Then it was baked (Danny was turned over and his bottom playfully smacked several times—one for each minute of baking). The whole process took about ten minutes, and daddy and Danny both enjoyed it immensely.

Betty's and Danny's parents probably thought they were just having fun with their kids. But they were doing much more than that. They were teaching their children how to play creatively. They were showing them that play is acceptable for adults as well as children, and that it can be fun for both. And they were showing them that creative thought can be expressed in play.

Creative people are often playful. They often describe themselves as being like children: playful and sometimes reckless. "When truly creative people come up with a new idea," said Dr. David Campbell, "they do not reject it immediately because of its flaws. They play with it, looking for strengths and sliding over weaknesses."

Howard, a friend of mine, likes to play creatively. Once he put a goldfish in the drinking water bottle at work. Everyone drank out of it and thought it was a big joke—except the boss. He drank out of it before he knew what it contained. He wasn't overly excited when he saw what he'd done.

Yet he was more than happy to put up with Howard's playfulness. Because Howard is very creative, and makes a great contribution to his company. His playfulness, even as an adult, is an evidence of his deeper creative ability.

As you read through this book, you'll see some evidences of playfulness. That's appropriate, I think, for a book on creativity. Playfulness *has* to be here to totally express the ideas. And it's inherent in the simple act of creating the book.

Things Parents Can Do

Too often parents assume the role of the boss with their children. Instead they should play with their children creatively. They should get down on their children's level and simply have fun with them.

One mom plays "mow the lawn" when she cuts her child's hair.

Another plays "motel" when she makes the bed.

Parents play tickle monster. They play horsy. They play Alice in Wonderland or Snow White or Wizard of Oz.

It's easy to make up other games or ways to play to help you in certain situations. For example, a wiggly child in church can have pretend glue stuck on his or her bottom to keep him or her stuck to the bench.

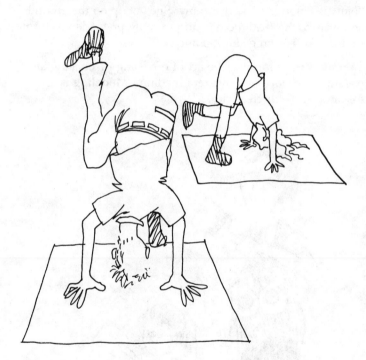

Here's something fun to play with children. Play the Twister game on a sheet of newspaper. Each person stands on his own paper, then twists according to the directions given: "Everyone put your nose and your left knee on the paper." "Everyone put your right foot and left hand on the paper." Take turns giving the directions.

Modeling

"Let's play house," said Jenny. "Okay," said Tammy. "I get to be mother. The rest of you can be the kids."

The children laid out the house—kitchen, living room, bedroom, and bathroom. "It's bedtime," said Tammy. "You sleep here. You sleep here, and you sleep here." She directed the other children.

"Now it's morning," said Tammy. She got up off the ground and went to the "bathroom" and promptly pretended to throw up just like her pregnant mommy.

Tammy was performing the act of modeling—recreating an experience or idea in a different medium. **Modeling is an essential skill for creativity.**

It's amazing how much children learn from copying (modeling) others.

Children play school, play house, play restaurant, and so forth. In doing so they model themselves after roles they see their parents in. The modeling helps them to better understand those roles. Other kinds of modeling involve actual models: model airplanes, cars, boats.

Scientists and technicians were able to envision today's rocket ships because of yesterday's toy rockets. The idea was simply expanded to send men and animals and equipment into space.

First attempts of people to fly were modeled after birds. People tried wings, feathers, and flapping, all trying to do what they saw birds do. The Wright brothers' first airplane was modeled after a toy their father gave them. Modern music is often modeled after classic pieces or harmonies from the past. Movies are models of real situations.

When Alexander Graham Bell was a boy, he made a talking machine modeled after a person's mouth and throat. He was able to get it to say such words as "Mama"—and the machine did it so convincingly that neighbors came over to see the new baby! When Bell invented the telephone, he did it by modeling the apparatus after the human ear.

Things Parents Can Do

Children will naturally be creative through modeling. But parents can help:

1. Give them play dough (either store bought or homemade) to model different objects of their imagination. One boy made an Indian encampment out of homemade salt dough.
2. Let the children make tents over furniture with blankets. These become playhouses, school rooms, teepees, dog houses, or camp tents, whatever the child wants to model.
3. Give children toothpicks and white glue and encourage them to "create." The results will be towers, teepees, houses, bridges, trucks, people. Or give them twigs, popsicle sticks, or something similar.
4. Give them toy telephones and other toy replicas of real items.
5. Have them build model cars, planes, boats, and so on.
6. Encourage role playing and impersonation as creative ways of "modeling" what children see and hear others do.

Drawing

"Hey, Mom! Look what I drew!" Craig grinned broadly as he stuck the picture under her nose.

"What in the world is *that*?" Mom asked. "I can't tell the top from the bottom."

"It's my dog," said Craig, a little less excited now.

"It doesn't have a tail," said Mom. "And his feet are way too big. Why don't you go try again?"

Drawing helps develop creativity and the imagination. But only if it's treated right. Craig feels pretty bad now. He thought he had done a pretty good job. But Mom thought it was dumb. Instead of being critical, perhaps Mom should have said, "That's neat! Why don't you explain it to me?"

There are other pitfalls to avoid too. Often children are given simplified pictures and told to color inside the lines. Or they are told to trace their hands and then put a beak on the thumb and turn the fingers into turkey feathers for Thanksgiving. These might be fun for a moment, but they don't help a child learn to draw—nor do they stimulate the imagination.

Drawing is important to creativity. It helps people to get their creative idea on paper so it can be better understood by all. It is one of the first steps to turning an idea into reality. When an idea is drawn out, it is easier to work with.

Things Parents Can Do

Some ideas to try:

- When your child draws something, be interested. And don't try to improve his work.

- Praise him for what he's done. Then, the next time you see a dog, point out how his tail wags, how bushy or slender the tail is, how big the feet are in relation to the legs. Pretty soon the dogs in your child's pictures will have tails. And the feet will be just right.

- But *don't* do this teaching at the time of the drawing. When your child creates a picture, the important thing is the effort, not the accuracy.

- Encourage your child to draw. Give him lots of scratch paper, crayons, water colors, and so forth. And before you know it, he'll be drawing as expertly as you do. Or, if you're like me, he'll be *more* expert!

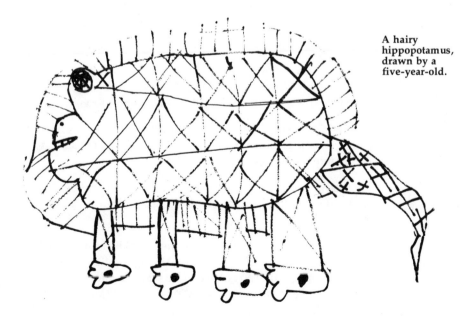

A hairy hippopotamus, drawn by a five-year-old.

Aim for One, Hit Another

The kids were getting bored. Nancy hit Rob and Rob squealed bloody murder.

"Why don't you play something?" Mom asked. "Don't you have anything better to do than fight with one another?"

"We don't know what to play," Nancy whined.

"Well, why don't you play—" Mom paused in thought. "Why don't you play like you're vacuum cleaners."

It was the right idea at the right time. Nancy took off, going through the room and scooping up toys and depositing them in the corner. Rob watched for just a moment, then took off in the other direction, making a sucking noise as he went.

Mom watched, astonished. It really was a good idea. And then: Aha! I can use this pretend game to good purpose!

The next time she needed the room cleaned up, she knelt down by Rob and Nancy. "Remember the vacuum cleaner game? Let's play it *together*! We'll suck up all the toys and put them in their box. Let's Hoover the house!"

Mom had aimed for one and hit another. Her objective was to give the kids something to do. But in the process she discovered a good way to get them to clean the room.

She was the happy beneficiary of a law of creativity: **often you'll be able to find a creative solution while you're seeking to accomplish something else.**

In another family, Ray spilled some crumbs on the kitchen floor. "Hey, don't be a slob," Mom said. "Clean up your mess."

When Ray got down on his hands and knees he found himself face-to-face with Butch, their dog. A light went on in Ray's head. "Butch, you're an anteater," he said. He directed Butch's head to where the crumbs were. As the dog licked up the crumbs, John made slurping noises.

Creative solutions come by making a connection between two different ideas. And often that solution will be different from what was expected.

When researchers started to look for a way to make a railroad lantern that wouldn't break in bitter cold, they hit their objective. But they hit another as well: they developed the excellent cooking and baking pots known as corning glass or pyrex.

Henry Ford aimed to go into the locomotive business, building steam engines and locomotive equipment. But in aiming for one, he hit another. He turned his creative energies to the automobile, strictly on the side—and ended up becoming the greatest car manufacturer of all time.

Space scientists turned their efforts to the difficult problem of how to insulate the astronauts in the extremely cold and extremely hot situations they'd be flying through. They were successful in their effort—but at the same time they hit another, developing some very useful materials for home building and insulated clothing. Space blankets and insulating tiles are just two examples of products that came from their work.

They also put their heads to work on how to make food for the astronauts: the astronauts needed something very compact and very easy to prepare. The scientists were successful, providing the astronauts with food that was tasty as well as nutritious. And they hit another creative solution, and the general public was able to enjoy such things as energy bars and powdered food.

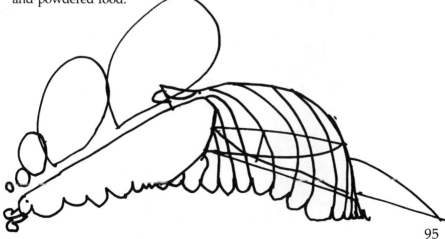

Things Parents Can Do

Parents can encourage their children to complete their creative projects even though the end result may not match what they started to make. A poem about flowers may end up about color. A picture of a horse may become a cow.

Children grow on praise, and they like to do more of the things they are praised for. When they find creative solutions to problems, praise should always be forthcoming—and then even more creativity will come forth. Let them try out their ideas, even when they seem foolish or ineffective. Often the creative effort is more important than the results.

"I started to draw a monkey—see the big ears—but it looks more like a lady in a long dress. But it's still a monkey."

Individuality

Benny was in the "terrible two's." Every time Mommy asked him to do something, he answered, "No!" Emphatically. He was beginning to assert his own individuality. He wanted to cut his own food on his plate. He wanted to dress himself.

One morning Benny walked into the kitchen with his shirt on inside out, his pants on backwards, and the heels of his socks on top. One sock was green and one was blue. "Look, Mama," he said. His brown eyes sparkled. He was feeling pretty proud because he had dressed himself.

But his mom could only frown. "You're dressed like a blind clown!" she said. "I guess I'll just have to dress you *right.*" And she did.

"Now pay attention so you can do it *right* next time," she said.

Creative people maintain a strong sense of individuality. They make their own decisions; they trust their own judgments. Creative people are individuals who stand on their own, who follow through. But what happens if all that is trained out of them while they're just kids? They lose a lot of their power to be creative.

Chestor Carlson, inventor of the Xerox copying process, is a good example of a creative, individualistic person. He persisted for 24 years after he had created his idea before he could convince others to buy and use it. He trusted his own judgment and persisted in spite of setbacks and problems. If he hadn't persisted, we might well not have photocopying today.

And that raises a good question: How many other inventions and compositions *would* we have today—but lost out on because the creator wasn't strongly individualistic? And another question: If your children become strong individuals, what will they have to offer?

Parents who want their child to be creative need to help him to be an individual who can stand on his own, who can be his own person, who doesn't need to have constant support, and who can be persistent, strong willed, know his own mind. Most kids will be all that automatically—unless their parents cause them to learn to be otherwise.

Things Parents Can Do

If children aren't strong-willed, they'll be unable to withstand the ridicule, doubt, and judgment of others. Most parents have success with these approaches:

1. Encourage the child to make his own decisions and learn consequences of the decision. "Which of these two outfits do you want to wear today?"
2. Let the child sometimes say "No," especially if he has a valid reason.
3. Trust the child's judgment—and show that trust by not interferring.
4. Allow the child to make his own mistakes.
5. Don't cover up for the child's mistakes—and don't baby him.
6. As the child grows, help him learn the socially acceptable aspects of individuality.

Check your child: Is he an individual who can stand on his own, is he his own person, is he able to get along without constant parental or peer support, is he persistent, does he know his own mind? Those are keys to develop in him if you hope to have a creative child.

Don't Scare Them Away

"Emily! What in the *world*?" Mother frowned and took in the scene: fingerpaint all over the kitchen floor, more fingerpaint on the cupboards, and still more on Emily. On the counter was a messy fingerpainted picture.

Emily looked up, a worried look on her face. "It's a picture of you, Mommy," she said, her voice quivering.

"Yes," Mother said, swallowing her exasperation, "and you've done a great job. Let's hang it on the refrigerator door, and then we can clean up this mess."

Too often parents see *only* the mess—the crayon marks on the wall, the glue on the table, the paper scraps on the floor, the clutter—and totally miss the creative effort of the child. In their anger they lash out at the child, not bothering to try to see what the child was up to.

The result is a stifling of creativity. **The more negative feedback a person receives, the less creative he will be.**

Take a look: The educational system usually considers creative answers totally unacceptable. One boy was taking a test that asked the question "Which of the following *don't* fly?" His choices: (a) birds, (b) butterflies, (c) fish, (d) none of these. He marked (d) as the answer—he'd seen "flying fish" on an ocean trip. But the teacher marked it wrong. He was, in effect, punished for his creative thinking. In many businesses, employees are criticized or reprimanded when their new ideas don't work out. It's not long before they stop trying anything new.

Creative people are often ostracized when they're perceived as "different." They don't fit the mold and are considered weird. This often causes creativity to stop. Children are no different.

Things Parents Can Do

Appreciation follows understanding. Try to understand what your child has made or drawn. It doesn't matter that it may not fit reality—it's the creative thinking that counts.

Try asking what a drawing or creation is. It may be completely different from what it looks like!

Here's a hard one: It increases creativity for a parent to allow her child to play in the mud and get dirty while being creative. Dirt will wash off—but the things the child learns will stay. If a child breaks or damages a tool when being creative, don't harp on the damage. Structure things so the child can work on projects without hurting tools or the house.

Don't give such constant criticism that the child becomes afraid of being creative.

"Boy, you really blew that drawing. Let me fix it for you."

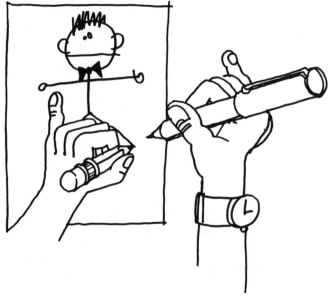

The Real Problem

What do parents do when they're faced with:

Temper tantrums
Bedwetting
Showing off
Hitting little sister
Sassing
Spilling water deliberately
Biting
Messing with dad's tools or mom's utensils
Slamming doors
Getting into mom's makeup
Dumping the wastebasket over
Playing in the middle of a newly planted lawn
Making silly noises
Turning the TV off and on
Turning the TV sound up super loud or very soft
Dawdling through chores
Talking to mom while she's on the phone
Butting in when mom is talking to someone else

Chances are that the parent will attack the problem head-on. And that will often be a mistake. Because those misbehaviors are only the *symptoms* of the real problem. They're not the problem itself.

Before the parent can truly solve the problem, he has to define what it really is. Maybe the child really craves attention. Or maybe the bedwetting is caused by a physical problem, which the child has absolutely no control over.

What's true with solutions to parenting problems is true with problems in general.

Creativity is often hampered because people try to solve the wrong problem. It's only when you define the true problem that you can solve it.

The city of New York once had the problem of passengers stealing light bulbs out of the subway trains. The *apparent* problem was that the bulbs were being stolen. But that wasn't the *real* problem. So the officials analyzed the situation, they realized what the problem really was: the people needed the bulbs to use in their homes.

Once they had defined the real problem they were able to attack it. Their solution: they reversed the threads on the bulbs, so they screwed in backwards.

The people soon learned that the bulbs were useless in their homes, and the thievery stopped.

Things Parents Can Do

When your child is faced with a challenge, it will do a lot if you can help him see what the real problem is. If he finds out that he's attacking the wrong thing, he can start over and do it right.

Try to do the same thing yourself, and your children will learn from you. Whenever you have a problem, try taking two steps back to get perspective.

Rest and Relaxation

Mother is always on the go. She's pulled from one end of the week to the other: a charity function, coaching a ball team, going bowling with friends, helping at the co-op preschool. *Then* the kids come home from school and the real busy-ness begins.

She'd like to take time to be creative. But where would she get the energy?

She'd like to be able to teach her children to be creative. But creativity requires a slower pace—and all mom's teaching is how to keep those legs moving on the treadmill.

Studies have shown that the ability to relax in our society has diminished greatly because of the stress and strain of modern life. Accomplishment, achievement, and striving towards distant goals are stressed to the point that rest and relaxation are considered counter-productive. That's unfortunate—because stress and busy-ness, and creativity just don't go well together.

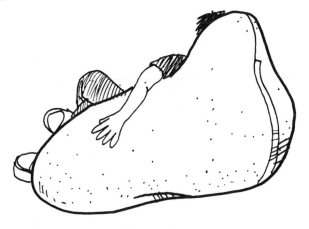

Kids love bean bags. They fit kids' forms and aren't easily abused. Bean bags are hard to top for rest and relaxation.

The ability to totally relax is directly related to a person's being able to create. Creative people work hard—then completely relax. This relaxation period often gives them their best ideas. Sir Isaac Newton was resting when the explanation for gravitation struck him. Henry David Thoreau developed some of his most profound philosophies while daydreaming by Walden Pond.

Wolfgang Amadeus Mozart said, "When I am, as it were, completely myself, entirely alone, and of good cheer—say, traveling in a carriage, or walking after a good meal, or during the night when I cannot sleep; it is on such occasions that my ideas flow best and most abundantly. Whence and how they come, I know not; nor can I force them."

Things Parents Can Do

Recognize the need for rest and relaxation, especially after hard work. If the parent is unable to do this, the children won't be able to either.

If parents change their pattern in life to allow for relaxation, their children will follow their example. *Rest* and *relax*. Your creativity will climb—and your children's will, too, as they learn the same habit.

Metaphorical Thinking

"Dad! Dad! It's raining styrofoam!" cried Billy. He rushed out the door and danced around. Of course it was really hail!

But Billy had no experience with hail. And he did have experience with styrofoam pellets.

When Dad came to look, he just laughed. "Don't be silly, Billy! That's hail, not styrofoam!" Then he went back to his newspaper—losing a good opportunity to help Billy grow in his creativity.

The effort to compare two different things develops creativity. This is called *metaphorical thinking*. Metaphors help us create new relationships by putting the words "is like" between things. Billy understood hail better when he got the idea that hail is like styrofoam pellets.

We humans need order in our lives. When we have an understandable framework, we can fasten new ideas and experiences onto it. We only understand the new when we can link it with our understanding and knowledge of the past. The more we can see "like" relationships, the greater the possibility we'll be able to come up with *new* solutions.

Many creative solutions come about by metaphorical thinking. George de Mestral created the velcro fastener—mating nylon tapes that cling to one another—by imitating nature's burdock burr. Shakespeare metaphors help us to see ourselves and our world in new ways.

Things Parents Can Do

So what can you do when Billy says the hail is styrofoam? Don't correct him—agree with him! Encourage him. "Yes, that does look *just like* styrofoam. It's called hail; it's little pieces of frozen rain." When your child thinks metaphorically, it will help if you think metaphorically with him. It will increase his ability to be creative.

Object Analogy

Strange noises in the kitchen—not encouraging to any mother. So mom goes down. All over the floor is a powdery substance. And all over the walls and the ceiling. On the counter the cocoa can (empty) and two Jello boxes (also empty). The kids look up when they see mom come in. One word describes their faces: horror!

"You kids!" she yells. "Look at this *mess!*" Later the story comes out: the kids weren't trying to be naughty. They were just trying to make dragon's breath, like they'd seen on the cartoons. They'd put the Jello and cocoa in their mouths, full, then blow it back out like smoke. It was great fun. They really did look like dragons.

Of course the kids didn't know how the dragon got his smoke. So they tried to come up with a creative solution of their own. They thought that the dragon's breath looked just like Jello floating on the air. And when they tried it, they realized they had their answer. Creatively.

The more you have the ability to see similarities between things, the more likely you'll be able to create a new solution. **Developing the skill to see similarities between seemingly dissimilar things will improve a person's creative abilities.**

There are numerous examples of this kind of analogous thinking. John Baessler got to thinking about the "buzz bombs" of World War II—and eventually developed the aerosol spray can.

Lewis E. Waterman saw in the capillary action of plants the "controlled leak" that became the fountain pen.

Chester Floyd Carlson saw in static electricity the ability to hold particles in place so they could be transferred to another surface. With that idea in mind, he invented the photocopying process.

Count Hilaire de Chardonnet saw the gooey mess of dried photographic chemicals—and stretched them out to make rayon, the first of many man-made fibers for textiles.

The following illustration shows a good way to use object analogy. People at a seminar were given the problem, "How can I improve my marriage?" Then they were instructed to use a pencil as an analogy to give them ideas. Here are some of the ideas they came up with:

Problem: How can I improve my marriage?

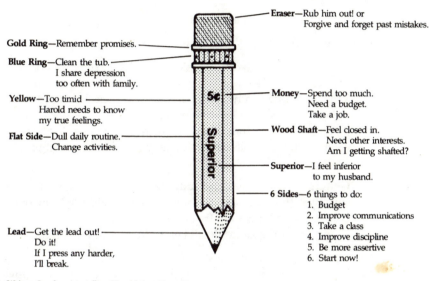

Gold Ring—Remember promises.

Blue Ring—Clean the tub.
I share depression too often with family.

Yellow—Too timid
Harold needs to know my true feelings.

Flat Side—Dull daily routine.
Change activities.

Lead—Get the lead out!
Do it!
If I press any harder, I'll break.

Write—Send a note telling Harold that I love him.

Eraser—Rub him out! or
Forgive and forget past mistakes.

Money—Spend too much.
Need a budget.
Take a job.

Wood Shaft—Feel closed in.
Need other interests.
Am I getting shafted?

Superior—I feel inferior to my husband.

6 Sides—6 things to do:
1. Budget
2. Improve communications
3. Take a class
4. Improve discipline
5. Be more assertive
6. Start now!

Things Parents Can Do

Parents can help their children see similarities between dissimilar items. And praise them when they try it on their own. Two little boys made roads and railway tracks from the roll ends of computer tape (inch-wide, black paper tape with holes punched in it). Three other children made balloons out of plastic surgical gloves. Another child cleaned dirt out from beneath her fingernails with playdough. The dirt stuck to the dough and came right out.

As children see the importance of similarities, they'll be able to solve many of their problems—and they'll become more creative.

Defer Judgment

Two five-year-old boys were sitting on the back porch. "I have a cardboard box that I'm going to make into a parachute," Vince said.

"It won't work," said Mike.

"It will if I . . . ," said Vince.

"Naw—it's a stupid idea," said Mike.

The more Vince tried to explain, the more Mike pooh-poohed the idea. There was one vital difference between the two boys: Vince was open to new ideas; Mike was critical and judgmental. Vince has a creative mindset, while Mike does not. And even though the parachute probably won't work, Vince's creative attitude will almost certainly lead him to another solution.

Getting creative ideas and judging their worth are two entirely different thought processes that should not be mixed. Newly formed ideas are fragile and imperfect; they need time to mature and acquire detail before they can be judged.

For example, when Chester Carlson, inventor of the electrostatic copy machine, tried to sell his idea, he met "an enthusiastic lack of interest." People judged his idea of little worth. But he didn't listen—and created the success story we call Xerox.

Fred Smith wrote a college paper about an idea he had: that of developing an overnight package-delivery system or service. His professor felt the idea was so impractical that he gave Smith a low grade. Fred developed his idea anyway—it's now become the multimillion dollar Federal Express.

Things Parents Can Do

When a child states an idea that the parent judges is impractical or won't work, the first reaction is to let the child in on parental wisdom. That should be avoided at all costs. Instead, hear him out, rather than cut him off. Then back off and let him try. If his solution doesn't work out, the parent should again hold back his judgment. The child will make his own, and learn from his effort.

What If? . . .

What if a car had legs? What if people could fly? What if trees could walk? What if water ran uphill instead of down? What if houses were round? What if we had eyes in the back of our heads? What if we were twenty feet tall? What if the sun fell on the moon? What if kids didn't have parents? What if giraffes lived underground? What if roads were made of rubber? What if books were made of salt? What if? What if?

"What if?" questions, constantly asked, drive you and me up the wall. "What if frogs married elephants? What if the sun didn't come up? What if you had noses on your hands?"

More than one parent has responded to all these what-ifs with one of his own: "What if I put a gag in your mouth?" Certainly you'd never do it—but the thought has crossed your mind. Right?

But inquisitiveness is the soul of creativity. Says Don Faburn: "If carried into adult life," the wonder and curiosity of the child "typifies the creative person."

There's a way to build that attitude: **Stretch the mind beyond known relationships, methods, and experiences.** The result will be a more creative person. If a person is able to wonder **freely** about "what if . . . " possibilities, then he will remain flexible and nonjudgmental. And he'll be more creative.

Children seem to wonder more naturally. Adults are usually too reserved and afraid to wonder "what if? . . ." David Campbell defines the stages we go through: "Age 7—Why? Age 17—Why not? Age 37—Because."

Children wonder naturally. It's part of their creative instinct. But here's a problem: too often parent's turn off their children's question tap. Down the drain goes the creativity. But what happens when inquisitiveness is let loose? Jules Verne asked. "What if man could visit the moon?" His ideas so entranced his fellowmen that a hundred years later men *did* visit the moon.

Buckminster Fuller asked, "What if we could design a more efficient building system?" Then he carried his question further: "What in nature is the most efficient structure in enclosing space with the minimum amount of materials?" His answer: the bubble. His inquisitiveness led to the development of the geodesic dome.

Things Parents Can Do

Parents can do a lot just by "playing the game" with their children. They can ask them "what if" questions themselves. That will show the children, very decisively, that "what if" is an acceptable way of thinking. It will show them that *the parent* does it as much as they do.

"What ifs" from the children must also be accepted. It's all in the state of mind—a parent can be constantly irritated, or can listen and enjoy!

Play pretend games: "What if I were a dragon and you were a princess? How would you escape?" What if you were a plant? How would you grow?" "What if I were a bird. How would I eat? What noises would I make?" "What if you were blind? How would you find your way around?" "What if you had purple skin? What color clothes could you wear to look nice?" "What if the sun were green? How would everything look?" "What if a giraffe had eight legs and his neck in the middle?"

Kids will always win at the what-if game. Take it as long as you can, though. It's a good creative exercise for growing minds!

"What if dogs could talk?"
"What if the ceiling was the floor and the floor was the ceiling?"
"What if we lived underwater?"
"What if our fingers had eyes?"

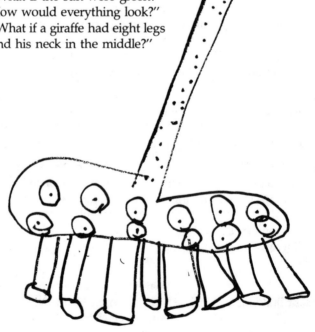

Hobbies and Fine Arts

Some hobbies are creative, but many are not. If you can have influence on the hobby your child has, choose carefully. **Doing and designing hobbies—not collecting kinds—can promote creativity and imagination.**

Some creative hobbies include:
painting and drawing
needlepoint
model making
wood-carving
metal working
macrame
furniture making
woodworking
photography
music performance (such as piano, flute, drums, guitar, etc.)
music composition
dance (including tap, ballet, modern)
knitting and crochet
flower arranging
writing
sculpturing
weaving
pottery making
jewelry making
silk printing or screening
making mosaics

Hobbies are great for developing creativity. And the nice thing about hobbies is that there are so many to choose from.

These hobbies help children develop the ability to be more creative. They contribute to and draw from the imagination and stimulate new ideas, solutions, and thoughts.

Discovery Can Lead to Creativity

Discovery is often the solution to problems—or it can lead to creative solutions. Edison invented many things by discovery. For example, the electric incandescent light came from his trying to make filaments—whether hairs, bamboo strips, cellulose, or metals—glow when heated white hot. His entire life was spent in the effort to discover creative solutions to problems. He had his own laboratory full of chemicals and apparatus at age nine.

One family, to help their children be creative through discovery, got a small microscope which they kept in the kitchen. Their eight year old was most fascinated by the things he placed under the microscope. One day he was looking at a grain of salt and asked for a paper and pencil to write down what he saw. He wrote down that it was square, clear, and crystal-like—much different from what he thought it would be. Another day he compared one of his own hairs, which was straight, with one of his mother's curly hairs.

Children often do things just to see what will happen. Read these examples—I think most of them will sound pretty familiar to you. In fact, you may wonder how I know so much about your family!

One boy filled the bathtub to overflowing just to see what would happen when it got to the top.

Another, in another family, plugged up the shower drain (they didn't have a tub) to see if he could make the shower into a tub.

A younger child took a whole roll of toilet tissue and flushed it down the toilet—not because he was naughty, but because he wanted to see what would happen.

Another child (this one not in the bathroom!) took two legs and a wing off a fly to see what would happen.

Every parent could record another score of examples from his or her own family—all instances of children learning and creating through discovery. How you act when your child participates in discovery will make a real difference to his creativity. If you get upset, and do it consistently, your child will still be curious about his world—but he won't be creative about it. He'll just be afraid to explore.

Things Parents Can Do

Parents can be very helpful as children use discovery for creativity. They can encourage them to discover the things around them and how they make our world a better one. They can show them leaves, bugs, rocks, cement being poured, cracks in sidewalks. They can talk about these things.

One father put a board on some dirt. In a few days, he and his children looked at the different bugs that crawled under it. After it rained, this father helped his children discover the different smells of the earth, the plants, and so on.

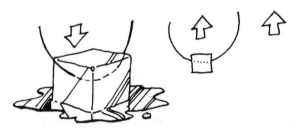

Some parents enjoy doing these experiments with their children to encourage discovery.

Press a strong wire down on an ice cube and hold it until the wire has gone halfway through the ice. Then you can pick up the ice cube with the wire—the pressure melted the ice enough to let the wire through, but then it immediately froze again, with the wire in the middle.

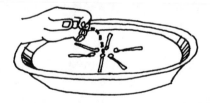

These are the kind of experiments kids love to try. They discover something new by doing them.

Fill a bowl with water, then arrange several matches in a star-shape in the center. Get a tiny piece of soap on a pin and put the pin in the center of the matches. The matches will all float away from the soap. Why? Because the melting soap changes the consistency of the water. The surface tension of the clean water floats matches better than the tension of soapy water.

The most important discovering a child will do will be on his own. Here the parent's role will be to *let it happen*. And a parent will often need to recognize that his kids will make a lot of messes in their efforts at discovery—and remember that they are simply being creative, not irresponsible!

Making It Real

"My children use more tape and string and glue than anyone I know," said one young mother to her friend. She piled a bunch of scotch tape in her grocery basket and started to reach for the masking tape.

"Well, my children sure don't," said the second. "I only let them have a little at a time. Tape and glue are so expensive and they don't need *that* much."

Guess which mother is doing a better job of helping her children be creative. . . .

I could rehearse the examples I've given you throughout this book and you'd see what I mean. What good would Edison's creativity have been if he hadn't *produced* his ideas? Newton *verified* his theories through experimentation and testing. If he hadn't, no one would have believed him. And no one would have benefited.

Then there's Bernie Schwann. Everyone's heard of him. He had the most creative ability of anyone on the earth, ever. He was an incredible genius when it came to creativity. Oh—there was only one problem. Bernie never produced *anything*. All his ideas just stayed in his head.

Thinking isn't enough, when it comes to creativity. Potential isn't enough. To be valid, creative ideas need to be *produced*.

You'll go a long way toward helping your child become more creative if you'll encourage him to produce his ideas. Get him to turn them into something tangible.

Children need to make things. Some of them turn out to be the strangest contraptions ever glued, taped, or strung together. **Ideas need to be verified by actually making the item.** After all, ideas are only thoughts until they have been produced. If children can't make the "things" of their imagination and ideas, they soon lose the will to be creative.

What if you allow your child to make things? You'll make a real difference in his development. It's a difference that will persist with him throughout his life.

Things Parents Can Do

A parent should seek to allow her child the opportunity to verify his creative ideas. It doesn't matter how dumb, how useless, or how impractical the idea may be—the fact that he has gone through the process of putting together and making the item is a very important part of creativity.

It's good to let children have the materials needed for verification. Keep a good supply of them on hand: string, tape, glue, paste, paper, sticks, etc.

Children can also verify their creativity in other areas, such as drama, music, and speech. Many parents enjoy letting them have opportunities for playing new tunes on the piano, giving a speech, acting out a part (with their own interpretation of it), making up their own plays, their own songs, and so forth.

Whatever a parent does, I hope she or he will be careful not to stop the children's verification because they make messes. Messes can be cleaned up.

Taking Away

"Let's have a luncheon like our mommies," said four-year-old Tina to her friend Marcie.

"Okay."

The two girls planned for several minutes and then asked Tina's mom for help.

"Can we use the TV tray for a table?" asked Tina, "and a towel for the table cloth?"

"Sure, " said mom. "Get your play dishes, and I'll fix some food."

Mom cut a sandwich into small pieces and then put some punch into a small plastic pitcher. The girls set their table with play dishes, put dandelions in the juice glass, and had a nice luncheon while their mothers enjoyed theirs.

Children naturally want to do what their parents do. They follow the examples around them. In doing so they often come up with some good creative solutions. **Their most common approach is to make things smaller, less complicated, with fewer parts, or more compact.** This approach is called *subtraction*.

Subtraction is a useful creative technique. Japanese auto manufacturers took over sales in the industry by producing cars that were smaller and more compact and used less gas.

Computers used to fill entire rooms. Through subtraction, table-top home units are now available that perform the same functions. Today, single computer chips have more memory capacity than the whole computer used to have.

By subtraction, G.E. has been able to increase the usefulness of light rays. By cutting down the length of the rays, they've developed heat lamps, ultraviolet lights, and lights that kill germs.

Things Parents Can Do

If a parent helps his child make existing things smaller or less complicated, he'll literally be teaching the child how to be creative. Try it—you'll like it!

Concentration

Creative thinking sometimes takes intense concentration. The ability to go into deep thought about a certain subject or idea is often essential to creativity.

Louis L'Amour, author of scores of popular western novels, is an example of someone who can concentrate deeply. He claims he can focus his concentration to the extent that he could write in the middle of a busy intersection without even being distracted. His level of concentration may be extreme, but he's a good model of what we should seek. His creative output is equalled by few.

"Jerry, hang up your coat, please," said Mother. Jerry didn't respond. He just sat there looking out the front-room window.

"Jerry, *please* hang up your coat," she repeated. But he just ignored her.

"*Jerry!*" Mother's tone was harsher. "Get that coat hung up!"

Still no response. So Mother walked over and grabbed his arm. "Now, young man, you hang up your coat," she shouted. "Don't you dare just sit there when I'm talking to you!"

Jerry stood up and went over to his coat. "You don't have to yell at me, Mom."

"I've been telling you for ten minutes!" she said.

"Oh, sorry," Jerry replied. "I didn't hear you. I've been thinking about how to fix my bike."

It sure looked like Jerry was ignoring his mother. But he wasn't. He was simply concentrating so hard that he had not heard her.

Things Parents Can Do

It can be very exasperating when your child ignores you—or appears to. But his ability to concentrate is a good creative skill. When your child is deep in thought, try not to get upset. Instead, give him some working room. You can get him to do his chores later.

Communicating and Creativity

"Hey, Mom!" Ann shouted. "I've got a great idea!"

"Tell me about it," Mom responded.

"Well, you take that one thing and you hook it up to the bigger one and they'll both work better."

"What things are you talking about?"

"You know—the ones in the garage. I don't know what they're called. Can you come help me?"

"How are you going to hook them together?" Mom asked.

"I can't really explain."

Ann is going to have a hard time getting help on her idea—she can't explain it well enough. The ability to communicate is an essential part of creativity. **Creators must be adept at communication** or others won't understand their ideas, solutions, or creations. Scientists and other inventors especially need to have communication skills—most lay people can't understand their jargon, and if they can't communicate, their ideas will often be unusable by the public.

Many forms of creativity—writing, singing, music, dance, art, drama—are actually methods of communication in themselves. The creator communicates both as the means and as the end of his effort.

Things Parents Can Do

Some things to try:

- Use toys and games that help children communicate. Try charades where pantomime is used to communicate, or a treasure hunt where effective communication is the key to the solution.

- Be conscious of how well your child is communicating in school and play. If there seems to be a problem, help the child isolate the communication problem so he can work on it.

- Children who have good role models for effective communication are more apt to learn good communication skills—kids mimic what the parents do.
- Hold family "show and tell" time. Each member of the family can show something to the rest of the family and explain all about it, answering any questions asked by other family members.
- Play a "touch-and-describe" game. Place different items in paper bags, then have the child touch an item and describe it without being able to see it.

Ideas Trigger Other Ideas

"What did you learn in school today, Tom?" Dad asked.

"We started a new reading book. It is the story of a dog and how he grows *up*."

"We saw *up* and *down* on Sesame Street," piped up three-year-old Troy. "*Up* goes that way." Troy pointed to the ceiling. "And *down* goes that way." He pointed to the floor.

"I saw a motorcycle really go *down* today," said twelve-year-old Bill. "A car didn't see it coming until almost too late. You should've heard the *brakes* screech!"

"That reminds me," said Dad. "I need to have the *brakes* checked on the car tomorrow. They seem to be slipping."

You've just seen an example of what one idea can do: **one idea can trigger a whole series of other ideas, all seemingly unrelated.** Even impractical ideas can trigger useful ones. It can be a very useful creative technique.

Consider brainstorming sessions you've been in. The thoughts get flowing so fast and furious they have to be recorded to retain them. And sometimes they even come too fast to hold onto them. As one person put it, the more the creative thoughts are flowing, the more continuous the creative thinking. This thinking is like a car. Once you get it moving, it's easy to keep on going.

Things Parents Can Do

Ideas, no matter how silly or useless, can trigger other ideas. Get your children talking. Ask a question. Then let the ideas flow. If you want to remember the ideas, write them down, or they may be lost forever!

Respecting the Child

"Hey, Mom! Look at my paper airplane!" shouted Stephen.

"Oh, I like that," said Mom.

"I made it all by myself."

"You did a great job. How does it make you feel inside when you make something all by yourself?"

"Pretty good!" said Stephen.

A few minutes later, Mom went into the kitchen. "Hey, I like the way you swept the floor, Loralee!" she said. "Thank you."

Loralee smiled. "Thanks, Mom."

When Mom tucked Anne into bed she kissed her on the cheek. "You sure helped me with the baby today. Thanks, sweetie."

Anne beamed.

None of these kids (except maybe Stephen) really did anything creative in this example—but their mother was building their creativity all day. She was showing them how she respected them.

Ways of Showing Respect

- Use praise.
- Be polite.
- Listen.
- Talk things over before punishing.
- Show lots of physical affection.
- Make sure the children understand that they must respect *you*.

Creative children have parents who value them as individuals. When a parent shows respect for his child, that increases the child's self-esteem. The more a child values himself, his abilities, and his thoughts, the more free he'll be to grow creatively.

Stories have been told of how the mothers of Einstein, Edison, and Alexander Graham Bell stood behind and supported their sons as they were growing up and experiencing difficulties. In short, they showed respect for the child; they built his esteem. Their efforts laid the foundation that enabled these men to reach their creative potentials in the years that followed.

For example, when Thomas Edison was eight he was enrolled in a one-room school, taught by a stern parson. A combination of dull teaching and a leather strap soon drove Thomas to the bottom of his class.

The teacher proclaimed that Thomas was "addled," and that he simply couldn't learn. But Thomas's mother, Nancy, had too much respect for her son to believe that. She withdrew him from the school and taught him herself.

The result—well, Edison's practical applications of electricity opened doors so that now I sit at an electric typewriter looking at a page illuminated by electric light!

Things Parents Can Do

It's important for parents to show respect for their child and his accomplishments. They need to acknowledge his efforts to be creative, show him they appreciate him as a person, and treat him with consideration. When he sees that he is a valuable person to them, he'll be more valuable to himself. That self-esteem will help him develop creatively.

Art, Dance, Music— and Creativity

"What are all these funny drawings on the wall here?" asked Aunt Jane.

"These," said Mother proudly, "are creative works of art by my children. This picture is by Jeremy, this one is by Bruce, and this one is by Annette."

"Oh. I didn't know they were artists." Aunt Jane was less than convinced.

"They may not be good artists yet, but they are very creative children. We put up new pictures every week and put the others in a scrapbook where we can look at them whenever we want to."

This mother enjoyed her children's creative abilities even though to others some of the drawings looked silly and immature.

Artistic ability is a skill. So are dance and music. Yet they are also creative media. **As a child has opportunity to experiment with these media, his creative abilities will increase.**

Art, dance, and music are all important forms of creativity. Not only are they creative mediums, but they develop valuable skills as well.

An artist is a creative person because he uses an abstract medium to express his thoughts and ideas. He begins with nothing and, using basic lines and colors, comes up with something.

Dance is also creative. The dancer uses his or her body motions and rhythms to express ideas and thoughts.

In music, abstract notes are used creatively to portray melodies, themes, and moods as conceived by the musician or the composer.

Things Parents Can Do

If possible, allow your children to use art, dance, and music to interpret their creative ideas and thoughts. Keep art materials on hand and allow your children to use them.

If it's feasible for your situation, let your children take art, dance, and music lessons. Through lessons, their skills will increase, and they will be able to use them to express their own creativity. And they'll become more creative in general, developing the ability to better express themselves in all areas.

Multiplication

Creative solutions are often found by multiplying existing things.

Car windshields had one wiper in the early days—but that was inadequate to keep the window clear. So car manufacturers found their solution by multiplying; they added a second wiper. But that still left the back window unclear. Multiplication again: some manufacturers are now adding a third wiper in the back.

Kitchen processing centers used to do one thing: blend ingredients together. Through multiplication, their number of functions have increased manyfold. Now they can blend, slice, dice, puree, mix dough, grind meat, and so forth.

Stereo systems have undergone the same transformation. They've gone from a simple turntable with speakers to the turntable, speakers, radio receiver, amplifier, cassette tape deck, and tape recording system. All through the simple idea of multiplication.

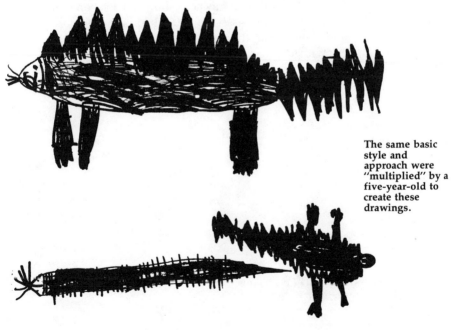

The same basic style and approach were "multiplied" by a five-year-old to create these drawings.

Mother pulled out her recipe book—and then pulled out her hair. The number of people at her supper had unexpectedly been increased from four to twelve. Relatives from out of town had dropped by. She quickly flipped through the contents of the book. Nope, no recipes for that many people. So she did the next best thing: she used the idea of multiplication. She found a recipe with ingredients designed for four people, then multiplied each of the amounts by three.

Amy was watching Mom make a small recipe into a large one through multiplication. The next day she was playing with her dolls, using a box as the doll house. But the box was too small. "Do we have any bigger boxes?" she called to her mom.

"No, only the small ones," came the reply.

So Amy used the idea of multiplication. She got several small boxes and put them side by side, each representing a different room in her doll house.

Things Parents Can Do

As you use the principle of multiplication in your home, take a minute and point out to your child what you're doing. Show her how one motor drives several items, how your food processor does several functions, how one kitchen utensil can be turned to many uses. As your child becomes more and more familiar with the idea, she will be more able to use it in her own life.

Honesty

Phil sat at the kitchen table, laboring over an abstract sculpture he was trying to make out of toothpicks and Elmer's glue. Things seemed to be going well enough—but suddenly he crushed his creation flat against the table and swept it into the trash.

"Why'd you do that, Phil?" his mom asked. "It was a beautiful sculpture. You were doing a wonderful job."

"Don't lie to me, Mom," he said. "It was ugly and you know it was."

Creative people usually have a high regard for honesty and integrity—even when it hurts. Phil knew his sculpture wasn't working out, and he knew that was obvious to his mother. He didn't want her to lie to him just to save his feelings.

The truly creative person sees the need for recognizing the truth about his work. If it's poor, he wants to know that; knowing his weakness will enable him to improve.

That desire for honesty and integrity carries over into other aspects of his life. He tries to see things as they really are. He tries to admit the truth even when he'd almost rather not.

The more honest a person is, the more he'll be able to see the true picture of the world. He'll have a clear, uncluttered view that will become the foundation of everything he creates.

The honest person will tend to seek the truth underneath appearances. For instance, if a man is careening wildly down the road in his car, one person will say, "Look at that drunk driver!"

But the honest and creative person won't jump to conclusions. He'll say, "Look at that man careening wildly down the road in his car."

Two people are seen kissing passionately. The first person says, "Those two are really in love."

The honest, creative person says, "Those two are really kissing passionately."

The difference is in how the creative person views the world.

He is interested in what's *true*. He recognizes that all in this world is not as it appears to be.

C. S. Lewis, a famed Christian philosopher and a highly creative individual, was well known for his honesty. He showed the value of that honesty in his *The Screwtape Letters*, where he took a look at things from the devil's viewpoint.

Things Parents Can Do

Always try to be strictly honest with your child. Tell him how you really feel about his creations. This doesn't mean you have to be totally negative—besides, that's not how you really feel, is it. You can be positive and still point out the truth: "Phil, I think I can understand why you threw that sculpture away. It just wasn't working out as a sculpture, was it? But did you notice that you're getting better and better in working with the glue? That's a valuable skill that will help you as you practice more and more."

In addition to being honest about creativity, a parent should be honest about everything else. That practice (and trait) will help the child be more honest with himself.

Emotional Climate

Andy was playing quietly in his room. "Andy!" his mother called. "Andy!" He came to the door. There was mommy standing at the bottom of the stairs, a frown on her face. "Andy, I told you two hours ago to take the garbage out to the cans. I'm tired of you not obeying. I can't believe I raised such a brat."

Andy reached for his milk at dinner. "Don't spill," Dad said. "You always spill."

In the middle of the night Andy wet his bed. He ran crying into his parents' room. "Make him sleep on it," his dad said, and rolled over.

But Mom got up, a frown on her face, and put on her slippers. "You probably do this because you hate me, don't you," she said to Andy.

Emotional climate. Andy didn't work on anything creative in the one day we saw him—but you can bet that if he did, it wouldn't be very good. There's a simple reason. **The more healthy the emotional climate in the home, the more creative the child will be.**

The opposite is also true, of course. And here we get a real insight into why Andy isn't creative: The more emotional stress a child labors under, the less he'll be able to do creatively.

More goes into emotional climate than the parent-child relationship. Also important is how the child feels about himself. Is he able to express his emotions freely—the negative ones as well as the positive? If not, he's being stifled emotionally. And he'll end up being less creative than the boy next door who isn't forced to keep his emotions pent up.

One family set up some rules to help the children freely "emote."

Rule 1: It's valid to express any emotion: love, anger, hate, sympathy, crossness, anxiety, fear, exasperation, whatever.

Rule 2: Emotions must be expressed verbally *only*. Hitting is not allowed, nor is throwing things or kicking furniture. If the child feels he needs a physical release, he is encouraged to go outside and kick a ball or kick the side of the house or run around the block.

Rule 3: In expressing emotions verbally, profanity is out.

Things Parents Can Do

To build creativity, parents need to establish an emotional climate in the home that will do two things for the children:

1. Help them feel loved and respected as part of the family. Help them to know that the parents care about them, that they trust them, that they want them to be happy.

2. Help them know that the parents care about their emotions, that emotions are okay to have and okay to express.

You can tell by the smiling, sunny, open feeling that this young artist has a good emotional attitude.

Point of View

"Lisa, will you dial Grandma's telephone number for me, please?" Mother asked. "I'll tell you the numbers."

Lisa dialed each number as Mother said it: 2 2 5 - 3 0 1 7.

A man answered the phone. "Joe's Garage. May I help you?"

"Mommy, it's not Grandma. It's Joe's Garage."

Mother grabbed the phone away and apologized to the man at Joe's. "I guess you're still too young to dial," she told Lisa.

She didn't even stop to consider that maybe Lisa *hadn't* made a mistake. There are two "O's" on a dial telephone—the number 0 and the letter O. Lisa had dialed the letter O instead of the number 0. Neither Mother nor Lisa was "wrong," but neither was "right." Their points of view were simply different.

Finding a creative solution or idea is often as simple as finding a different point of view. By seeing another point of view, a person can see new ways of solving a problem.

Dr. Alvin Price at Brigham Young University used the idea of point-of-view shift to teach the meaning of motherhood to young women. He asked each girl to buy a raw chicken egg and use it as her "baby." She had to clothe it, find sitters for it (or take it everywhere with her), bathe it, pamper it, and so forth. Through the shift in point of view, the girls were able to see more clearly the problems a real baby poses. Dr. Price's creative teaching method utilized a change in point of view to get the message across in an effective way.

Things Parents Can Do

Parents can be creative by helping their child see and use other points of view. One way for the parent or child to experience what it's like to see things from a different point of view is to bend over and look at things through their legs. The world looks different upside down. Flaws in the paint, dirty spots, colors, and the like become more vivid, more intense. You tend to notice different things in the same surroundings. Why don't you try it and see how different things appear?

Ask First, Judge Later

Billy interrupted Dad's reading of the evening paper. "Dad, what's 2 and 2?"

Dad answered without looking up. "4."

A few minutes later, Billy came back. "Dad, what's 2 and 2?"

"Hey, I told you. It's 4! Now let me read."

But Billy persisted. "2 and 2 isn't 4."

"Then what in the world is it, Mr. Smart Stuff. If you know the answer, don't come bothering me!"

"I don't know the answer," said Billy. "I wanted you to tell me."

A minute later Billy came back, holding a piece of paper. "What is 2 and 2?" He pointed at the number. The answer was 22. The 2s were next to each other.

Children often see things from a different point of view than their parents. That causes problems. A child may be approaching a problem from his own point of view, and the parent will think he's all wrong. Instead, the parent should shift *his* point of view. **Refrain from judging another person's idea or approach until you're certain you know where he's coming from.**

"No-no!"

Judgments by a well-meaning parent usually come too early and too much. And they end up stifling creativity.

For example, H. G. Booth, the inventor of the vacuum cleaner, arrived at his solution by looking from a different point of view. A device had been invented which would blow dirt away (because that particular inventor reasoned dirt could be blown rather than swept with a broom). H. G. Booth saw from a different point of view. He made a device which would *suck* the dirt into a container.

Things Parents Can Do

Some suggestions:

- Whenever your child tries an approach that seems stupid to you, try not to judge him. He may simply be operating from another point of view. There's an old Indian saying: "Never judge your brother until you've walked a mile in his moccasins."

- Let your child's natural creative urges go—don't try too hard to direct or correct him. His point of view is just as valid as yours—it's only different.

- Creative solutions will almost always be different when approached from different points of view. If you can learn to see things from the view your child has, you'll be able to be more tolerant and more helpful.

- Just as an experiment, crawl around the house for a while to to see what things look like from there. Look at things from upside-down. Lie on the floor and stare up at the ceiling; look around and see what you can while you're flat on your back, without rolling over.

- Things look different from different points of view. And when things look different to you, you'll react differently. Your creative solutions will be different. If you *never* expect your child to have the same creative solutions as you would, you'll probably be right!

"What is this little monster thing, Johnny?"

"It's grass with bumps on it, Dad. Can't you tell?"

Family Influence

Right after supper Meg's mom had to rush off to a class she was taking. Her dad sat in his favorite chair with a new book, something about how life was when George Washington was alive. Meg moped around for a minute, trying to decide what to do—then she got a book of her own to look at on Daddy's lap while he read his.

After a few minutes Dad put his book down and grasped the side of Meg's book. "Here," he said. "Let me read this story to you."

Chances are that Meg is a rather creative child. **Creative people usually have models of others who are constantly learning new things, who are continually seeking new stimulation.** Most creative people found those models at home, with their own parents.

Meg's mother is always going to the library, and Meg gets to go too. Her mom picks out several new books to read. Meg gets some too. And throughout the year her mom usually goes to at least one class a week. She's not letting her brain stagnate. She's excited about herself and the world around her. She likes to learn, and she's willing to pay the price to make it happen.

Meg's dad is also a good model. He brings books and magazines home from work and pores over their pages. He gets books from the library, too, on a wide variety of subjects. Meg can tell that Daddy likes to read—he has to because he does it so much.

Mom's and Dad's attitudes about learning can't help but rub off on Meg. She sees learning and exploration as a natural, desirable thing. The result is that she becomes more and more creative as she grows in that environment. Her brain has more data to create with as she continues to learn. And the constant stimulation automatically gives her creative new ideas whenever she's faced with a challenge.

The highly creative Margaret Bourke-White, an internationally known photographer, talked about the importance of family influence in her autobiography, *Portrait of Myself:* "Learning to do things fearlessly was considered important by both my parents. Mother had begun when I was quite tiny to help me over my childish terrors, devising simple little games to teach me not to be afraid of the dark, encouraging me to enjoy being alone instead of dreading it, as so many children and some adults do."

Things Parents Can Do

If you would have a creative child, seek to be a model of constant learning. Use your library, or build your own from bookstore purchases. Read the books you have; let your brain be stimulated; set an example of excitement about learning. That example will rub off on your child. Children want to be like their parents—you can help them be a "likeness" that's creative.

Another important thing parents can do is to practice the ideas in this book. Perhaps that goes without saying. Moms and dads should joke with their kids, play with them, make things with them, let them be individualistic, let them go through the processes of discovery. Moms and dads should consciously seek to do a good sampling of the things this book recommends. That will be a family influence for creativity that will have effects throughout the child's life.

If one member of a family is creative, it's likely that the entire family is developing good creative abilities.

Summary Checklist

It's our belief that the best way to help a child be more creative is to be familiar with good creative approaches and skills, and then to use them at the opportune moment. Here is a checklist of all the concepts covered in this book. *Enjoy!* Creativity is not work, it's fun!

- ☐ **Creating "On Demand"** Trying to force creativity brings only one thing—nothing! Truly creative things can never be produced on demand.

- ☐ **Abstraction** Creativity becomes easier when one starts looking at things in the abstract.

- ☐ **Too Much Freedom** Setting limits on a child's creative activity doesn't stifle him—it enhances!

- ☐ **Getting in a Rut** Let your child fall into an habitual way of doing things and he'll cease finding more creative ways to walk through life.

- ☐ **Kinds of Junk** Who needs fancy equipment—kids can be creative with just junk!

- ☐ **Reading** *Alice in Wonderland* and *National Geographic* can open a child's mind—and get his creative juices flowing.

- ☐ **3-D Thinking** Thinking three-dimensionally is an important creative skill. And it's one that can be learned.

- ☐ **Picture This** Creative people are usually able to picture things in their minds. It's a vital skill—one that can help turn dreams into realities.

- ☐ **Convergent Thinking** Take many ideas and bring them together for one solution and you've got convergent thinking.

- ☐ **Brainstorming** Families can work together to produce a bunch of creative ideas. Then the kids can try them out.

☐ **Switching Things Around** Kids can learn to be creative by rearranging things: switching them around to find different approaches that work.

☐ **Kinds of Tools** Tools make the crucial difference between thinking about something and making it happen.

☐ **Experiences and Creativity** Creativity is often the combination of things we know about. The more a child learns through experience, the more he can combine.

☐ **Combining Things** Bring together two things that don't normally fit together and sometimes you have a third thing that's completely new.

☐ **Hatching an Idea** Creating is like hatching an egg—sometimes you have to sit on an idea for a while before it's ready to hatch.

☐ **Checklists** The mind is a wonderful tool, but only when it's used to capacity. Checklists help a person look at all the angles; they help him cover all the bases.

☐ **Hunches** Millions of great creations have come "just on a hunch." Kids get hunches too—and they should be encouraged in them.

☐ **Getting It Down** Creative ideas must be recorded in some form or they'll vanish.

☐ **Experts and Specialists** Don't think a child has to be an expert in something before he can do creative things. In fact, if he *isn't* an expert, his mind will probably be more open to all the possibilities.

☐ **Adaptation** Creativity doesn't just mean coming up with new things all the time. It's equally creative to *change* something that already exists.

☐ **Positive Approach** Creations are made by building up, not tearing down. "Any jackass can kick a house down, but it takes a carpenter to build one."

☐ **A Sense of Destiny** Some kids feel they have to "do or die"—they have a sense of destiny about their mission in life. They feel they *have* to create; something from inside is driving them on.

☐ **Learn to Question** Every kid asks "Why?" "What is that?" It can drive a parent nuts—but it also opens the door for creative thinking.

☐ **Division and Omission** Take something away, or divide it in half—both are good approaches to creativity kids can try.

☐ **Small Rewards Can Cause Creativity** Kids like to be rewarded—who doesn't? But make the reward the right size or it might just cause problems.

☐ **Need Fosters Creativity** "Necessity is the mother of invention." If a child wants to do something bad enough, he'll find a way.

☐ **The Real Solution** For every problem a kid has, he can usually think of a bunch of solutions. But he won't really be creative until he picks the *right* one.

☐ **Complex or Simple?** Some people like things simple. Some like them complex. If your child prefers the complex, he's likely to be more creative.

☐ **Divergent Thinking** Take one idea and find all the ways it can be applied: that's divergent thinking.

☐ **Develop Holistic Thinking** Kids can be more creative when they look at the whole problem, not just isolated parts.

☐ **Trading One for Another** Substitute one part for another one and you've got something new.

☐ **Dreams** Thomas Edison got a lot of his ideas through dreaming. Your child might be able to do the same.

☐ **Mother Nature and a Good Idea** We can learn more from the fish or the firefly than it might seem at first glance.

☐ **Order and Tradition**   Some parents like to act very "proper and dignified." That makes for a formal atmosphere. It also makes for a child who's less willing to be creative.

☐ **Turning Things Around**   Sometimes doing things backwards will bring the best results of all.

☑ **Games and Puzzles**   Some types of games and puzzles can get a child's imagination going.

☐ **Adding To**   When a child is stuck with a problem, he can try adding to. Putting new things with the old ones will often bring the solution that's needed.

☐ **"Great Job!"**   The more parents encourage a child to be creative, the more creative he'll become.

☐ **Seeing It in Your Mind**   Learning to see in the mind's eye things that don't exist—but could—is an important creative skill.

☐ **Hard Work**   No one ever becomes truly creative without putting in a lot of hard work. Kids who know how to work are more likely to be a success at creating.

☐ **Accept the Unpredictable**   Children will do a lot of unpredictable things as they creatively try to discover their world. Mistakes need to be tolerated (as much as you can!).

☐ **Multiple Skills**   Most creative people have several skills. The more things a child learns to do, the more creative he'll be able to be.

☐ **Don't Take Things Too Seriously**   Kids will make mistakes as they learn to be creative. A sense of humor (in the parents!) helps greatly.

☐ **Preconceptions**   Should a vacuum blow out? It will if the inventor has preconceived notions—but it won't work. The preconceptions we bring to our problems invariably stifle our creativity.

☐ **"I Can't!"**   It's hard, if not impossible, for a child to be creative when he doesn't think much of himself.

☐ **Modification**   When a child has a problem, and he needs a creative solution, he doesn't always have to come up with something totally new. Often it's more effective (and more efficient) to modify something that's already there.

☐ **Environment Promotes or Kills Creativity**   Kids respond to their environment. If things are set up for them to be more creative, they'll be more creative. But environment can kill it too.

☐ **Playing Around**   The tickle monster and the guy who puts goldfish in the drinking water bottle have one thing in common: they both have the playfulness it takes to promote creativity.

☐ **Modeling**   Kids will naturally copy things they see as they express their creativity. But there are ways their parents can help.

☐ **Drawing**   Drawing helps develop the imagination—even if a child can't draw a house with four walls.

☐ **Aim for One, Hit Another**   Often the result we're shooting at isn't the one we hit. But we end up with something better than we'd hoped.

☐ **Individuality**   Kids who are allowed to really be themselves end up the most creative of all.

☐ **Don't Scare Them Away**   Criticism kills creativity.

☐ **The Real Problem**   If a child isn't able to identify what the real problem is, he'll work forever and still fail to come up with a good solution.

☐ **Rest and Relaxation**   Creative people know when to push hard and when to go into neutral. But just because your child's eyes are closed doesn't mean his mind is empty.

☐ **Metaphorical Thinking**   Comparing one thing to another—thinking in metaphors—is a good creative technique. In creating something, making a good metaphor is like building a house from a good set of blueprints.

☐ **Object Analogy** Using an analogy is as good as finding your ideas are really pure gold.

☐ **Defer Judgment** It's easy to judge, but harder to create. Both parents and children should refuse to judge the merit of an idea until it's been given a chance.

☐ **What If? . . .** Let your mind go: What if birds were made of stone? What if my face were made of plastic? What if we could smell through our fingers?

☐ **Hobbies and Fine Arts** Hobbies don't always come cheaply—but they're excellent ways to develop creativity.

☐ **Discovery Can Lead to Creativity** When your child flushes a roll of toilet paper down the toilet (or tries), he's not being naughty. He's only trying to discover what will happen. And, like it or not, he's being creative.

☐ **Making It Real** Ideas are worth about what they weigh until they're turned into something concrete.

☐ **Taking Away** Some of the best creative ideas come from subtracting parts of existing things.

☐ **Concentration** Call until your throat is sore—it won't do you any good if your child is creatively concentrating.

☐ **Communicating and Creativity** The better a child becomes at communication, the more effective he'll be in his creativity. A lot of creative media *are* communication; other ideas need to be communicated for people to appreciate them.

☐ **Ideas Trigger Other Ideas** When a child gets stuck and doesn't know where to go, you can get him going on another idea. Ideas trigger other ideas—and he may end up where he wanted to be in the first place.

☐ **Respecting the Child** If a child feels that his parents respect him, that they value him as an individual, he'll feel more free to grow creatively.

☐ **Art, Dance, Music—and Creativity**   Art, dance, and music all require skill. Yet they're also creative mediums. Children who get opportunities to experiment in these will end up more creative in general.

☐ **Multiplication**   Take one thing and turn it into many. That's multiplication. It's also a good approach to finding creative solutions to problems.

☐ **Honesty**   Really creative people are usually scrupulously honest about their creations—and they expect the same from those around them.

☐ **Emotional Climate**   The more healthy the emotional climate in the home, the easier for the child to be creative.

☐ **Point of View**   Finding a creative solution or idea is often as simple as finding a different point of view.

☐ **Ask First, Judge Later**   Don't judge a child's idea until you're certain you know where he's coming from.

☐ **Family Influence**   Creative children usually have parents who are constantly learning, who enjoy creativity themselves. Or who at least respect it in others.

Answers

Don't use the pieces of paper to make a square—use them to define the outside edges of the square.

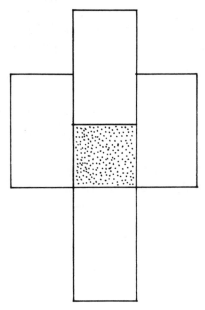

Push your partner's string *under* the loop on your wrist. Then slip the loop over your hand and you are free.

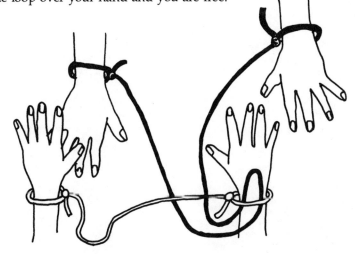

143

Bibliography

Design Yourself!, Kurt Hanks, Larry Belliston, Dave Edwards—William Kaufmann, Inc.
Take the Road to Creativity and Get Off Your Dead End, David Campbell—Argus Communications
Put Your Mother on the Ceiling, Richard de Mille—Viking Press
Training Creative Thinking, Gary A. Davis—Holt, Rinehart and Winston, Inc.
Conceptual Blockbusting, James L. Adams—W. H. Freeman and Co.
The Metaphorical Way, William Gordon—Porpoise Books
Synectics, William Gordon—Harper and Row Publishers
Experiences in Visual Thinking, Robert McKinn—Brooks/Cole Publishing Co.
On Knowing, Jerome Bruner—Belknap Press
Applied Imagination, Alex Osborn—Scribners
New Think, Edward de Bono—Glencoe Press
Fire of Genius, Ernest V. Heyn—Anchor Press/Doubleday
The Universal Traveler, Don Koberg and Jim Bagnall—William Kaufmann, Inc.
The Art and Science of Creativity, George F. Kneller—Holt Rinehart and Winston, Inc.